THE MIDDLE PATH—
THE SAFEST

THE RELIGION OF "HEAD AND HEART"

> "Evolution has brought us down to this material plane that we may learn valuable lessons. The experiences we are garnering are qualifying us to enter greater and more sublime fields of activity. It is hoped that this little volume will convey another message that truth is not limited to any special sect; hence whoever subscribes to the creeds and dogmas of organization, automatically shuts off his power for independent thought."

S.R. Parchment

ISBN 1-56459-790-3

Request our FREE CATALOG of over 1,000

Rare Esoteric Books

Unavailable Elsewhere

Alchemy, Ancient Wisdom, Astronomy, Baconian, Eastern-Thought, Egyptology, Esoteric, Freemasonry, Gnosticism, Hermetic, Magic, Metaphysics, Mysticism, Mystery Schools, Mythology, Occult, Philosophy, Psychology, Pyramids, Qabalah, Religions, Rosicrucian, Science, Spiritual, Symbolism, Tarot, Theosophy, *and many more!*

Kessinger Publishing Company
Montana, U.S.A.

Preface

THIS little volume is the outcome of a series of four lectures given on the subject, "The Middle Path—The Safest," by the Author, at the San Francisco Rosicrucian Fellowship Center.

These lectures were well attended and appreciated beyond expectation, and the constant demand for articles on this important subject has prompted the publication of these lectures in one volume.

There is an ever increasing number of people who think that to be spiritual, one must, like the Buddah, renounce the world.

Although seclusion may be sought at a certain stage of one's unfoldment, renunciation of all material duties is absolutely unnecessary while going through the nine initiations of the Lesser Mysteries.

Evolution has brought us down to this material plane that we may learn valuable lessons. The experiences we are garnering are qualifying us to enter greater and more sublime fields of activity, thus we should not scheme to play truant from this school of life.

Matter is the negative pole of Spirit and in a way may be considered "crystallized Spirit." Thus thrice great are those who renounce their eternal happiness in order to work for man's redemption.

It is hoped that this little volume will convey another message;—that "Truth" is not limited to any special sect; hence whoever subscribes to the creeds and dogmas of organization, *automatically shuts off his power for independent thought.*

In accordance with the words of the Buddah, quoted below, this volume is sent forth to accomplish its mission.

"Accept nothing that is unreasonable; discard nothing as unreasonable without proper examination."

S. R. PARCHMENT.

EXPLANATION OF CHARTS NOS. 1 AND 2

Occult and Scientific investigations have proven beyond all doubt that the laymen of primitive races did not know the Planets—Neptune and Uranus. Such a knowledge was reserved by the Custodians of the Sacred Science, having been revealed to esoteric students only. Since the vibrations of these two orbs were too attenuated to affect the ordinary man, the "Serpents" made no mention of them in religious ceremonies.

In Chart No. 1 the white triangle represents the spiritual sun, from which the physical sun of our system, and the suns of all other systems emerge. In other words, occult science teaches that the visible sun is the field of evolution for Beings vastly above man and is not, in any sense of the word, the Father of the other planets, as material science alleges.

Beside being the home of the Dhyan-Chohans or Archangels, it also serves as a focussed lens through which the tremendous energy, and the powerful light of the CENTRAL sun, are diffused through the seven planets which march around the "Solar Logos." Therefore in all religions, we hear of the Seven Planetary Genii,—for, hath not the poet said:—

"The Seven Spirits before the Throne
    To The Lord All-Mighty pray.
The shining orb of day responds
    With stimulating ray.
They pray for Wisdom, the Cosmic Christ
    Shines forth from the Central Sun
In love divine all life is bathed
    All life—there is but one!
One life, one will, one Wisdom,
    One grand eternal plan,
One Author of the Universe,
    One brotherhood of man."

The Egyptians chanted mantrams of Seven Vowels which was directed to the Seven Ruling Intelligences; the Hindu tells of the Seven Rishi; the Mohammedan of the Seven Archangels; the Parsi of the Seven Ameshaspentas; the Christian Religion has its Seven Spirits Before the Throne; and in Occultism the "Seven Schools of the Lesser Mysteries" are also recognized.

The exoteric student who has not earned the right to know the ray or Planetary Genie to which he is attuned, finds himself at variance with the religious views of others; many such students become philosophical tramps, and assistance is of little value until they cultivate stability of purpose. They are, so to say, in darkness, and must so remain until the marriage of the higher-self and lower-self has been consummated.

On the other hand, the esoteric disciple, when conscious of the "Ray" to which he vibrates, and whose inner vision, or Christ consciousness, has been awakened, is attuned to the mellow light of Rā. (See Chart No. 2.) Only such a pupil is able to peer through the "Golden Light" of the Cosmic Christ, and behold in aspirants of other Rays—"The Infant Logos"—for, by the Christ that is formed in him, can he behold the "Christ" in others. His head, so to say, is drenched in the effulgent light of the Logos of his own being. He therefore becomes conscious that the Seven Planetary Genii, and all the beings that are evolving through them, are indeed but children of one common Father. Such a disciple is said to be vibrating "In tune with the Infinite."

In other words, as the Physical Sun, and all the other planets of our system are vibrating in unison with the Spiritual Sun, in like manner the Golden Light—"The Magic Mantle," which the Mystic has woven, attunes him to all mankind; the Son of man becomes a Son of God. Thus:

"HE WHO SEES THE TRUTH, IS NEITHER OF THE EAST NOR OF THE WEST—HE IS OF GOD."

THE MIDDLE PATH—THE SAFEST

Sequel to

"Step To Self Mastery"

THE MIDDLE PATH—THE SAFEST

The Middle Path of attaining spiritual illumination was instituted and taught by Gautama Buddha approximately 600 years B. C. History informs us that this great soul was the son of a ruling monarch. Although he was of noble birth and was heir to great luxuries, yet in early life Gautama renounced wealth and fame because he discovered that happiness could not be derived from mundane things. It should be evident to all of us that worldly possessions can give but fleeting pleasure—never happiness. Yea, even though our environment be the most secluded, and even though bedecked with the things which are most costly and beautiful, if we are void of intelligence to constructively use the things we possess, we would most certainly be miserable beings.

History tells us that because Gautama's father discerned in his son the strong traits of the ascetic, he tried in every conceivable way to influence the lad to take interest in the pleasurable things of life and in the duties of state. It is also recorded that in the king's effort to distract his son's attention from spiritual studies, he built for the young prince beautiful mansions at various resorts. At these palaces dancing maidens of most ravishing beauty were employed to entertain the young prince.

It is one of the traditional customs of the East Indian races for parents to arrange the marriage of their children. Thus in conformity with this age long habitude, Gautama was married when but a child. But all the monarch's efforts utterly failed to dissuade the young prince. no one of these influences causing the youth to change his mode of thinking. He was firmly convinced that only by the attainment of spiritual illumination could one be most successful in assisting suffering humanity. The call of the spirit, which usually manifests as the "inner urge" was so impelling that Gautama eventually forsook all material possessions and became a wandering monk.

It is almost beyond the conception of average humanity, to perceive how impressive must have been the inner voice which impelled a prince to renounce wealth and worldly honors and don the robe of a wandering monk. The response of Gautama to the higher call, beside being an inspiration to the whole of humanity, should be of special benefit to Christians, for in it is contained the true meaning of the saying of Christ Jesus: "NO MAN CAN COME TO ME, EXCEPT THE FATHER WHICH HATH SENT ME DRAW HIM . . ." St. John, Chapter 6, verse 44.

The theological interpretation of this saying

is that the Master referred to an anthropomorphic God, an outside Diety, who is separate from the indwelling spirit or God within. This false doctrine, brought about by the many erroneous theological interpretations of the Master's teachings, has been instrumental in keeping the people in ignorance. The laity has been instructed to believe in a personal God and a personal Devil. These negative ideas which are vividly impressed on the minds of the people, have caused the great masses to believe that man is but a "worm of the dust." These false beliefs have completely stripped the Ego of all potential God-given attributes —yea, even qualities which we have meritoriously acquired, are said to be special gifts from God.

It is the writer's belief that negative religious ideas have been the cause for the large percentage of human derelicts among us, and the time is not far distant when the governments of the world will be forced to institute laws against the promulgation of negative religious doctrines, the same as they have enacted laws to safeguard the people against dope peddlers and bootleggers.

It is very evident that, should this step be taken and this policy impartially carried out, it will be the best method of teaching the arrogant masses Self-Reliance. When the reason for the indolence and backwardness of the people is sought, the unbiased investigator is usually convinced that the spiritual psychology of the people is in reality the main one. Thus, peddlers of negative religious doctrines are prime factors in depriving the people of the primal initiative quality. After the study of thousands of cases it has been discovered that a man can easily be saved from the liquor and dope habits; while on the other hand, after the mind has been doped with a negative religious teaching, and the "worm-of-the-dust" doctrine has been implanted in the budding mind by trained psychologists, it ofttimes takes more than one earth-life for the Ego to regain the primal creative power which it has surrendered. Few, indeed, can be induced to look squarely at facts and believe that each man is his own redeemer.

Because of the numerous negative religious doctrines which are continually being meted out, the greater percentage of humanity is daily pouring out supplications to an anthropomorphic Deity instead of relying on the God within. The blind ignorance in which such people are existing, mistakenly described as "childlike faith," has sapped their vitality and rendered them incapable of coping with conditions of mundane existence. Thus, in blind ignorance and extreme sentimentality, they continue to offer selfish supplications to a personal God, and are supinely waiting on "Jesus Christ the only Begotten" to be their redeemer. But:—

"No answer comes to those who pray
  And idly stand,
And wait, for stones to roll away

THE MIDDLE PATH

  At God's command.
He will not break the binding cords
  Upon us laid
If we depend upon pleading words
  And do not aid.
When hands are idle, words are vain
  To move the stone;
An aiding angel would disdain
  To work alone.
But he who prayeth, and is strong
  In faith and deed,
And toileth earnestly, ere long
  He will succeed."

Buddha taught that each man is his own redeemer, and every student of the Esoteric Doctrine believes this statement of the Master to be absolutely true. The doctrine which the great sage taught is revered by all truth-seekers, because it is based on logic and offers the only reasonable solution for the many perplexing problems of life. Truth-Seekers also know that Christ Jesus did not refer to an exterior God when he said, "No man cometh unless my Father calleth him." Several chapters of the four gospels bear witness that the teachings of the Master Jesus were identical with the Buddhistic doctrine. Christ Jesus taught a positive doctrine and admonished his followers to believe that they were "Gods in the making." But after the death of the Master his followers canonized him as the only Son of God, and they have declared that the door of redemption was closed to all but the chosen few, who believe in the "Immaculate Birth" and "Cleansing Blood" of Christ Jesus.

Every student of occult science who has attained illumination knows that the "Father that calleth" is the aspirant's Higher Self, the God within, the birthless and deathless evolving spiritual spark which has neither beginning nor end. Every student of the esoteric doctrine knows that man is a spark from the Divine Flame and has created for himself both a physical vehicle, and his own peculiar environment by means of which he is garnering most valuable experiences. The old adage "Experience is our only teacher" is one of the unadulterated aspects of Truth. Knowledge garnered by experience acts as pabulum to the evolving Ego, and is the only means by which the impotent Spirit can attain omnipotency.

The Ego is slowly but surely becoming a self-conscious creator. Spirit in its primal state is a negative abstraction of the absolute and each spark inherently possesses all the qualities of the Primal Flame; but in order to become "Self-Conscious Creators" each spark must pass through every cycle of being, culminating in its highest aspect on earth in man. The Ego that we call "Gautama Buddha" was very far along on the path of evolution at the time of his reincarnation. It is said in esoteric parlance that he communed with his mother before conception. She beheld the incoming Ego clothed in the vestment of a Monk, and in his hand was a fresh-blown lotus flower—the symbol of Purity.

Sceptics may consider the spiritual experience of Buddha's mother the result of the vivid imagination of a demented brain. But if we are to consider the experience of a cultured Rani an hallucination, it would not be justice to exempt the parents of Samson, John and Jesus, as they had similar experiences. The hierophants of exoteric Christianity claim the spiritual experiences of the parents of John and Jesus were "special favors conferred by God," but the thinkers believe that the just laws of Nature, which we call God, bestow no favors. What we are and what we have, are results of our own actions.

If therefore, the spiritual experience of Sakyamuni's mother is to be considered a state of hallucination, the parents of John and Jesus must also be catalogued as sufferers of dementia praecox.

Occult investigations have proven that when an Ego has attained to full-waking-consciousness, it is given the opportunity of selecting its parents; and if the parents are also spiritually awakened, the incoming Ego often establishes communication with them months, and even years, before the time is ripe for conception. In the near future all advanced parents will self-consciously contact the egos that are seeking embodiments through them. The truth is, there are at present many parents having such spiritual experiences, but as the leaders of Christendom teach that at "every birth a new soul is created fresh from the hand of God," the spiritual experiences of advanced souls are usually repudiated and, if they were to insist upon the authenticity of their visions, very rarely would they escape the insane asylum.

Those that have such experiences usually consider their revelations too holy to be lightly discussed. Thus they have adopted the Virgin Mary's method and "ponder the mysteries in their hearts." By personal experience of contacting the egos of their children, many parents are convinced that the doctrine of Reincarnation is a universal law and is not a heathenish belief, as is taught by Christian theologians.

History informs us that Gautama's parents were not the only ones who knew that the ego which reincarnated was of a high spiritual order. Students of the Stellar Script that were versed in the law of cycles, knew that the time was ripe for the appearance of a great teacher. The seers and wise men (or Nagas) of the realm were all cognizant of His coming, and at the birth of the Babe, many of these sages came and prostrated themselves before the parents and child and predicted that the young one was destined to become a Buddha. Many of the prognosticators advised the monarch and his wife, that if they desired the child to take the reins of state, precautions should be taken

THE 7 SPIRITS BEFORE THE THRONE

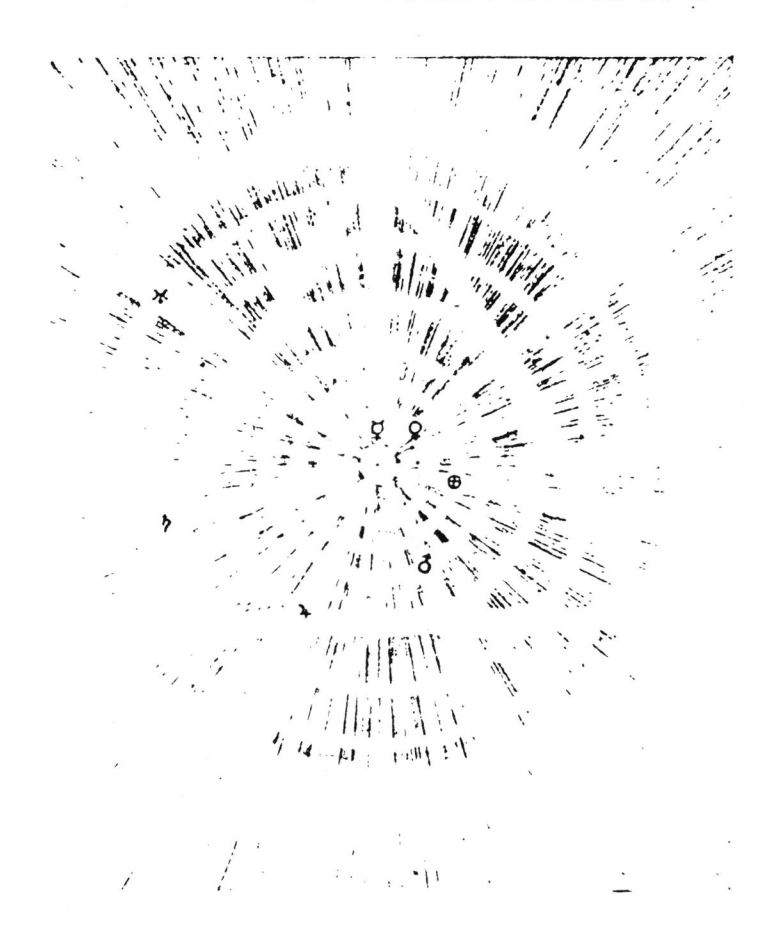

DIAGRAM 1

that the child did not come in contact with suffering humanity during the years of maturing.

The father, who was longing for a son to reign in his stead, willingly accepted the advice of the sages and, to prevent the prince becoming an ascetic, special care was taken to have his education be along lines that would qualify him to cope with the practical duties of state. It can readily be seen that, though the motive which prompted the Maharajah to discourage the prince in his spiritual pursuit was not for a selfish purpose, the former, nevertheless, was used by the invisible forces of Nature, to become the unconscious tempter of his beloved son.

But as the inherent ascetic qualities which he was endeavoring to crush out of the prince's consciousness, could in no wise be snuffed out or appeased by wealth, fame, honor, or any earthly pleasures, the spiritual flame which the monarch had succeeded in only temporarily suppressing, reasserted itself and impelled the prince to go to the extreme. He renounced all worldly wealth and honor; had the hair of head and face shaven, donned the saffron robes, and went forth from a palatial environment to the homeless life, completely frustrating the plans of his parents.

It is said that during the years which Gautama spent in quest of truth, he tried every available means before attaining success. Undaunted in his search he created a new system, and by his own methods he finally attained enlightenment. Hence it is said he is the "Discoverer of the Undiscovered Path."

In the western world we dedicate statues to our great men. These images remind us of the noble deeds which the pioneers of the race have accomplished, and ofttimes we are inspired to walk in the footsteps of the departed saint, warrior or scientist whom we have immortalized in clay or bronze.

For the same lofty purpose the Eastern races are prompted to dedicate statues to their great sages. Thus there are statues showing Gautama in rags,—begging bowl in hand; there are images portraying him after his long fast as a living skeleton; there are numerous idols depicting him practicing rigid oriental austerities which are too shocking to portray to occidental minds, and in like manner there are images portraying his attainment of full enlightenment.

After Gautama had attained at-one-ment with the Christ Principle, with the spiritual eye of a Buddha, the wise one distinctly perceived that the mentality of the masses was not sufficiently evolved to understand the great mystery of creation. In the Pali Canon for instance, mention is made that He declared that He "Could not teach the Norm of Norms to Man;" Christ spoke to the multitude in parables, but revealed the meanings to his disciples; and in like manner, Paul the Christian initiate, gave the simplest teaching, or the "Milk of the doctrine to the babes in Christ," but to the more progressive, he gave "meat" or the more advanced teaching. Thus the Buddha admonished rigid self-restraint, which is the "meat of the doctrine," for the disciples who were in earnest, by which to free themselves from the wheel of birth and death; but to the masses, the wise one gave only the "milk of the doctrine," instituting thereby the "Middle Path" which he declared the "safest" for the multitude.

Students of comparative religion can readily discern the golden thread of truth which unites all religions. The Christ's Sermon on the Mount conveys the same spiritual truths as does the Buddha's first discourse, commonly known as the "Dhammachakkappavattana Sutta," translated by Rhys Davis as the "Setting in Motion of the Royal Chariot-Wheels of the Kingdom of Righteousness." It is also described in Buddhist literature as the "Turning of the Wheel of the Law." In this sermon the Enlightened One explained for the first time the "Four Noble Truths" and the "Noble Eightfold Paths," including The Middle Path.

In St. Paul's Epistle to the Phillipians, a most practical and constructive admonition was given: "Let your moderation be known to all men." This statement shows clearly that Paul was also an advocate of the "Middle Path." Nature is ever striving to attain perfection; and a rounded development should be the goal of the aspirant; if students of occult philosophy would strive with greater zeal to practice moderation in all things, in a few short years they would in a normal way quicken the slumbering Christos within and start the self-conscious struggle to free themselves from the wheel of Rebirth.

There are many aspirants seeking enlightenment through the "Doctrine of the Eye"—the mere reading of books. It should be remembered that Gautama, Jesus, and all those that have attained illumination did not acquire their wisdom in colleges, nor in special temples of worship, nor indeed, had it been gratuitously conferred upon them.

The Arahats of every school of thought have unanimously agreed that, although the "Doctrine of the Eye" is very helpful during the early stages of unfoldment, "Self Forgetting Service" is, nevertheless, the shortest, safest, and most joyful way to final liberation.

It is the consensus of opinion of those that have attained spiritual illumination that the "blissful state cannot be fully attained while we are functioning in a vehicle which is subject to disease and death." It is very evident that health, wealth and temporal power may for a while give a phase of contentment, but never happiness. Nay, prolonged contentment is not even the portion of those who have attained illumination, and the reason for dissatisfaction is very obvious, for, if happiness could be realized on this mundane sphere, very little progress would be made, inevitable stagnation and absolute crystallization would be the outcome.

Thus the aspirant in whom the Divine Fire

is awakened, does not crave contentment. He knows only too well that ease and comfort are but pleasure grounds for the senses. These he seeks to avoid. Contrary to the ideas of the great mass of humanity he considers discontentment a great asset, yea a blessing in disguise, for by discontent alone can he move on to better things.

Onward, upward and forever onward is the battle cry of the conquering spirit. The discerning eye can easily behold it, seeking expression in every department of Nature; from the clod to the God the divine fire is present. Thus by the innate urge we continue in our struggles until we shall finally be lost in an effulgence of glory which is beyond the concept of finite mind.

But mark this, the struggle is carried on instinctively in all the lower kingdoms of nature, and by the animal man. The self-conscious struggle begins when we enter the Occult Path, and when we, so to say, have broken away from exterior leaders and started to serve the God within. In occult parlance those that have taken such a bold step are said to have "Entered the Stream;" in other words, they have by their own volition entered the Path of Regeneration and are seeking to attain the superhuman stage, and freedom from the wheel of birth and death. He who has attained this state, has by his own merit, become one of the Saviours of the World. Such a one is called in esoteric parlance a "Stream Winner."

During the disciple's struggle for liberation,

grave dangers beset his path. On every side he is surrounded by pitfalls. Lust for wealth, fame, power, and the abuse of the procreative force are usually considered Waterloos for many a promising student. But I say unto thee, O Traveler, the most deadly pitfall for the beginner is the vacillating mind which leads to seeking those teachers who promise quick results. It is commendable to be of an open mind, but it should be strictly understood that an open mind is not synonymous with an ever-vacillating attitude. The open minded person may be very stern and fixed, but if upon observation and analysis a principle conforms to reason, he will accept it, while on the other hand the vacillating attitude whch by many is considered liberal-mindedness, has caused the great masses to be roaming from one teacher to another.

As a bee in quest of honey flits from flower to flower, so there are thousands of so-called truth-seekers running from one school of thought to another, and the truth is that along physical, mental, and spiritual lines such students are making very little progress. As a matter of fact the man who is strictly orthodox and believes his special little doctrine to be the only right one, is at least developing fixity of purpose, while on the other hand, if the student of occultism has not unfolded the prerequisite qualities of self-reliance and stability of purpose, he is destined to become a derelict on the ocean of life.

The advice of those that have attained illumination is sure to be of inestimable value to the young aspirant, but pay heed, O Pilgrim, to another of the priceless gems of the Lord Buddha:

"Believe not what you have heard said; believe not traditions merely because they have been transmitted through many generations; believe not merely because a thing is repeated by many persons; believe not conjectures..., believe not solely upon the authority of your Masters and Elders. When upon observation and analysis, a principle conforms to reason and leads to the benefit and welfare of all, accept it and hold it."

Judging from the illuminating and reasonable advice which Gautama gave his monks, Buddhism could in no wise be considered a religion based upon blind faith, and of all the religious doctrines, it is considered the most logical. By the critics of the Western World it is designated a religion based wholly on metaphysics. Its chief mission is, nevertheless, the blending of head and heart, and the mere fact that its followers have never shed the blood of man or beast, should be sufficient proof to convince these sceptics that the heart unfoldment was in no wise neglected in its teachings.

All religions have as their fundamental principle the saving of men's souls. The modes of worship of the savage tribes although unintelligible to civilized society, are nevertheless best suited for the evolution of the peoples that are attracted to such crude forms of worship. As a man evolves, his concept of a ruling intelligence changes in like degree. Thus, the Deity of the savage is usually a God of vengeance, a Being whose wrath can be appeased by the fumes of incense and chanting prayers; and among the most savage races even human sacrifices are offered to appease the wrath of their Deity. Although civilized society has made great strides, the paganistic idea of an anthropomorphic Deity with the human attributes of love and hate, is still their firm belief. Thus in time of war we find the religious leaders of Christendom blessing the sword of one race to inflict punishment upon another. The reason for this is, the majority still believe that God can be coaxed by sweet smelling incense and prayers to change His mind. On the other hand the true enlightened occult investigator believes not in a personal God, but in a universal Principle, a law which pays no heed to prayers and incantations. This class is endeavoring to live in harmony with the Primal Cause which Principle of Law and Order manifests in every atom of the universe. Consequently in spirit and in truth they worship the Divine Intelligence of Nature.

However cruel a religious doctrine may seem, it nevertheless is playing an important part in the great scheme of evolution, and the golden thread of Truth which runs through all teachings can be distinctly seen by every student of the secret doctrine. Thus in like manner can the aspirant of the esoteric wisdom-religion enter a sanctuary of idols in India and worship with the devotees; if he is in Rome he may worhip at St. Peter's Cathedral; if he is with Naturalists, he can enter the devotional attitude and may use for a Shrine, a beautiful oak, a flower or a thistle; in other words, he belongs to the universal Church of God and sees Deity in all things.

The followers of exoteric Christianity are instructed that "Jesus is the only Begotten Son of God," and they are forcibly impressed with the idea that "Whosoever believeth in this Divinity and the cleansing power of His most precious blood, shall be saved; and those who do not believe in the Christian creed are doomed to everlasting damnation." The doctrine of Buddhism is the antithesis of exoteric Christianity. Gautama taught that the Ego is a spark from the Divine Flame and that man's redemption is in his own hands; hence he is a potential Deity. Buddhism teaches that when a member of the human life-wave has attained enlightenment, — in other words, — after one becomes a "Buddha" or a "Christ", he is qualified not only to be a teacher of mortals, but he has also merited the high office of instructor of Devas, Chohans and Gods. The idea of man becoming a teacher of the celestial hosts is considered blasphemous by orthodox

Christians, who from birth have been taught that "Man is a worm of the dust". It can readily be seen therefore why it is not an easy matter for those who have been instructed in such a narrow belief to conceive the possibility of man evolving to that exalted state, which entitles him to the high office of instructor of the heavenly hosts.

In recent years the advanced educators of Christendom have been advocating the doctrine of evolution, but the mere teaching of evolution without also accepting the doctrine of rebirth, is insufficient to satisfy the inquiring mind. Force and matter, or spirit and form, are, so to say, inseparable. Matter is the negative pole of spirit, and matter and spirit are evolving pari passu.

Occult Science teaches that it is the indwelling spirit that creates both its own form and environment. It can readily be seen that the acceptance of the doctrine of rebirth would mean the shattering of the entire structure of exoteric Christianity, and to offset such a catastrophe, the crafty leaders have designated all peoples as "heathens", who believe in reincarnation.

Mention has already been made that all religions are fundamentally the same, but the esoteric side of the Christian teaching is known only to the few that have outgrown the dogmas of organized sectarianism, and the Powers that are behind the various established denominations are making no effort to emancipate the minds of the people from the erroneous tenets which the hierophants, who preceded them, have taught. If the foregoing is a truthful statement, how then could the ignorant masses which have been instructed only in the exoteric side of their religious faith, and whose minds are dominated by fear of eternal damnation, be otherwise than apprehensive in exchanging religious views with other races?

Through the lack of spiritual insight the races of the Western world have misconstrued the lofty and holy teaching of Gautama Buddha. The fundamental principles on which the doctrine of Buddhism is established are as follows: First, the evolution of the spirit through repeated embodiments; second, the sacrificing of selfish interests for the good and welfare of all; third, unlike the Christians' belief in a "personal Saviour," Buddhism teaches that immortality must be attained by one's own merit.

"The Middle Path is the Safest," declared the great Reformer. Thus if those that have adopted the Buddhistic faith have erred and strayed from the "Middle Path," it is unjust to point to the East Indians and affirm that their backwardness is the result of their religious belief. The aspirant acquiring mental development, yet is lacking in the wisdom of the heart, to guide him aright in his quest for truth, is like unto a ship without a rudder on a stormy ocean. It is logical to conclude that such a craft would eventually meet its

THE MIDDLE PATH

doom. Thus, in like manner, a nation that is lacking in a rounded development is also doomed to meet destruction.

It is said in occult parlance that: "Even ignorance is better than head-learning with no SOUL-WISDOM to illuminate and guide it," which the occult student understands to mean,—THE AWAKENED HEART.

Soul-wisdom ofttimes manifests even in those that have no education; while on the other hand it rarely manifests in those that have acquired only an intellectual unfoldment.

The student possessed only with head-learning, is destined to become entrapped, and eventually will be lead away a captive by his own imaginings. Head-learning or mere intellectual development without the awakening heart, will in the end lead the disciple into the left-hand path of black magic.

Wisdom may be attained by the development of the heart alone. Nevertheless, it is advisable that aspirants should endeavor to unfold equilaterally, for the crowning glory of Soul-Wisdom usually attains its greatest efflorescence among those that have awakened both head and heart. Thus individuals as well as nations should ever bear in mind that the "Middle Path is the Safest." H. P. Blavatsky said: "The Mind is the slayer of the Real. Let the disciple slay the Slayer." We are living in the "Age of Reason," and mind seems to have both slain and devoured the germ from which the faculty of "Spiritual Perception" should have grown. The few devoted disciples that have "Slain the Slayer" and by so doing have developed "Spiritual Perception," can see the golden thread of Truth in all religions. Thus, they are endeavoring to inaugurate a universal doctrine, and further the brotherhood of man.

In the Christian bible there are several passages which are in absolute accord with the tenets of Buddhism, but these priceless gems of truth have been misinterpreted and distorted to suit the whims of the various sects into which the Christian doctrine is divided. And since the Christian faith is segregated into more sects than any of the other existing beliefs, it can readily be seen that complication is more acute among the followers of the gentle Nazarene. In several instances the spiritual meanings of passages of scripture are veiled in such jargon of words, that even the hierophants are unable to decipher their true meanings. Thus until the scales of superstition and ignorance are removed from the eyes of the missionaries we are sending into foreign fields, and until the races of the occidental world sheathe the sword and cleanse their hands which are scarlet with innocent blood, we shall never be able to interest the teeming millions of the Orient; nor can we ever hope to convert the adherents of the only bloodless religion, founded by Gautama Buddha, 600 years B. C.

One of the many aspects of truth known to all students of the esoteric doctrine is: that all religions are fundamentally the same, and if the leaders of the various sects were not so hopelessly blinded by selfish motives, the religion of Universal Brotherhood could, in a few decades, become a reality. Buddhism is considered atheistic by many, but if those that are denouncing the great faith were sincerely looking for the oneness of Truth, they would readily discern in the Christian scriptures that Christ Jesus, like the Buddha, also believed that "Man is an evolving Deity."

Apropos, the emphatic statement of the Master as recorded in the Gospel of St. John. Chap. 10, verses 22-39, may help to verify the statement which has been made, and the following is gleaned from the story:

At the feast of dedication, Jesus walked in the temple, and while in Solomon's porch the Jews came unto Him with many questions. During the conversation Jesus declared, "I and my Father are one." The Jews, knowing Him to be the son of Mary and Joseph, declared that He blasphemed, and were about to stone him; but the Master, being versed in the religious doctrine of his own race verified his statement by saying: "Is it not written in your law, I said Ye are Gods?" It is most obvious that, on this momentous occasion, the Master was endeavoring to bring to the notice of the Jews one of the most vital points which was being ignored in their religious doctrine; but, blinded by ignorance they could not understand. They were taught only the "letter of the law" which suppresseth the truth. Thus for His good deeds they sought to stone Him.

As it was in the time of Christ, so it is today; ignorance is reigning supreme, for though we boast of our great accomplishments, we are, nevertheless, adhering to many pagan customs. As a matter of fact, in many instances the interpretations of the holy Scriptures by our so-called men of God, are mere jargons of words which are pregnant with paganistic ideas and void of intelligence. It is evident that the brief and positive statement, "I and my Father are one," and the passage quoted by the Master, mean the same. Such gems of truth need no interpretation whatever, but we have been juggling with words, and instead of upholding the positive side of Christ's teachings, the hierophants are promulgating a negative belief, and even in this enlightened age the "worm-of-the-dust" doctrine is still being taught.

IN THIS great country, many of the executives of states have been influenced by selfish religious leaders, to enact laws for the abolishment of the teaching of evolution from the curriculum of Public Schools. It is very obvious that the steps which are constantly being taken to suppress the truth are for no other reason than to keep the masses in ignorance concerning the God-given-power within.

If in the hope of saving the Christian religion, we are forced to encourage ignorant pagan ideas, then my prediction is that exoteric Christianity is destined to crumble. We may for a while be succussful in influencing the people to see themselves as "worms of the dust," but this spell cannot last forever. Slowly but surely the indwelling spark of Force in each human being will be fanned into flame by "Evolution." Thus, if the leaders of Christendom refrain from teaching the positive side of the Christian doctrine, when Evolution will have matured the Indwelling Spirit of a sufficient number of truth-seekers, these enlightened souls will be drawn together by mutual attraction, and wage war to free mankind from religious despotism.

Since the Doctrine of Evolution has only recently been accepted by a few educators of the Western World, it is apparent why many followers of the various Christian denominations believe that all anti-christians are doomed to eternal damnation, and although blinded by ignorance and in greater need of spiritual food than the socalled heathens, they still continue to support the mission work in foreign fields, which is at best reaping but a fruitless harvest.

In the innermost consciousness of every believer of Buddhism is the grounded belief that "Man is an evolving Deity;" yea, although poor and miserable, his belief gives him buoyancy and fortitude. His faith teaches that by individual action, or by the slow process of evolution, each human being shall some day attain Buddhahood, and final liberation from the "Wheel of Rebirth."

"Striving to be Man, the worm
  Mounts through all the spires of form."

No one can deny that great gulfs exist between the degrees of culture of the various races; but he that is earnest in quest of truth should endeavor to overlook petty differences. For, until the aspirant has evolved to the degree which lifts him above the spirit of the clan, never can he be trusted with the Sacred Teachings, which are designed to qualify him to intelligently direct the forces of Nature. He who is seeking to become a "Knower of the Truth" must "Neither be of the East nor of the West—he is of God." Instead of our continued search to discover the differences existing between the religions of the various races, we should strive to look for consonances, and when enlightened by the gems of truth which we have discovered, we would then be qualified to erect a solid foundation upon which the religion of esoteric Christianity, or Universal Brotherhood, would forever stand.

Max Muller truly has said: "There never was a false God, nor was there ever really a false religion, unless you call a child a false man." It is evident, the underlying motive of all religions is for the "enlightenment of man," or in other words, we may say the primary motive is for the "saving of men's souls." Thus, however crude or even brutal a religious doctrine may seem, it is nevertheless playing an important role in the great cosmic plan, by assisting the evolution of the class of egos that are attracted thereto.

The most rudimentary knowledge of evolution is usually of sufficient importance to convince both sceptic and sincere truth-seeker that, through the slow process of evolution, man, with the numerous celestial hosts, eventually will become Gods. The investigations of all schools of occult philosophy are found to agree that there are varied gradations of beings beyond the human. Thus the egos which constitute the life wave to which the angels belong are one spiral above the human; the arch-angels are one spiral above the angels, and two spirals above man. The spiral mounts ever upward; therefore, by reason's torch one can readily see that there is a life wave composed of the Higher Gods to which the Deity of our Solar System belongs.

Looking backward from the human life wave, it is very obvious that man is one loop of the spiral above the animal; the animal life wave is one spiral above the plant kingdom, while the mineral kingdom, which is one loop below the plant, is rooted in the Cosmic-Root-Substance—the Divine Source of all things.

The study of evolution reveals to the aspirant that in every department of Nature there is progress. In other words, not only must man be considered an evolving God, but in like manner every atom is a potential Deity, indicating that there is wisdom, wisdom everywhere,—so grand, so beautiful, that words are inadequate to convey half of what unfolds before the spiritual vision.

Since the spiritual impulse travels in the spiral path, it is evident that conditions of no two life-waves could ever be the same. Although the hosts of heaven have passed through conditions similar to our own, never were they clothed in bodies composed of dense physical atoms. As we can learn much about Africa by reading the works of noted explorers of the dark continent, or by conversing with an intelligent native of that country, in like manner, when the regenerate man returns to spirit life, he is every whit qualified to instruct the celestial hosts whose evolutions have not entitled them to wear coats of skin.

In the occult philosophies of the East, life on the physical plane is said to be the greatest limitation for the spirit. In other words, while the orthodox Christians believe in a post-mortem hell, the students of esoteric philosophy know that earth life is the greatest hell. In the sacred teachings it is also made clear that, "When man has merited freedom from rebirth, he is received among the celestial hosts with the greatest honor."

Our language is inadequate to describe the grandeur of the reception which is given the redeemed man. H. P. Blavatsky, a faithful student of Eastern Masters, in the "Voice of the Silence" (that mine of Occult Wisdom and priceless treasure which she has given to the world), has attempted to portray the joyous welcome which is given the "Stream Winner," in the following words:

"Behold, the mellow light that floods the Eastern sky. In signs of praise both heaven and earth unite. And from the four-fold manifested Powers a chant of Love ariseth, both from the flaming Fire and flowing Water and from sweet smelling Earth and rushing Wind. Hark! . . . from the deep unfathomable vortex of that golden light in which the Victor bathes, ALL NATURE'S wordless voice in thousand tones ariseth to proclaim:

Joy unto ye, O men of Myalba.
A pilgrim hath returned back 'From the Other Shore.'
A new Arhan is born.
Peace to all Beings."

End of Part One.

PART TWO

It is the concensus of opinion of all those who have earned the right to behold the sacred and mysterious workings of Nature, that the things which are spiritually conceived can not be accurately explained in words. Not until after the disciple has proven that he can exist independent of his physical body in full waking consciousness, not until after he has by personal experience proven that his house of clay is but a temporary dwelling, can he fully comprehend and appreciate the attempts which have been made by Mystics to express in words their experiences of the things which are spiritual. Towards our knowledge of man's future existence, the Initiates of all races have contributed voluminously; but Gautama Buddha, and the Jewish Initiate, Christ Jesus, have done more than any of the others to spiritualize humanity. Gautama has given to us the vistas of truth of the ego's continual reincarnation, and its final liberation in the following words, which may appropriately be called "The Buddha's Chant of Liberty."

> "Through many a round of birth and death I ran,
> Nor found the builder that I sought. Life's stream
> Is birth and death and birth, with sorrow filled.
> Now, house-builder, thou'rt seen! No more shalt build!
> Broken are all thy rafters, split thy beam!
> All that made up this mortal self is gone:
> Mind hath slain craving. I have crossed the stream!"

The perusal of historical records has proven that of those who have attained enlightenment, none other has made greater sacrifices than Gautama Buddha. Although he was a prince and even though the selfishness of parental love caused his father, who became tempter, and tried every possible means to induce his beloved son—the heir to his throne—to desist from his quest of truth, the call of the Spirit was too forceful, too compelling, and could not be set aside. Thus contrary to his father's wish, Gautama renounced the royal robes and crown of state. In humility he had the hair shaven from his head and face, donned the saffron robes of the monk, and with begging bowl in hand, went forth from a palatial environment to the homeless life.

During the years which Gautama spent in quest of Truth, he studied the various philosophies of his native land. After he had exhausted every available means he was still dissatisfied: knowledge he had acquired but "wisdom" was wanting. Fired with a determination which no obstacle could conquer, he decided to use his own creative ability, which resulted in his discovering the Inner Light—the Adi Buddhi. Judging from the unbiased advices which Gautama repeatedly gave his disciples, it can readily be seen that the Holy One had extracted the Cream of Knowledge from all the teachings which he had investigated, and adding these informations to the wisdom he inherently possessed, Cosmic Wisdom flowed into him and he became a Buddha. After attaining true spiritual insight, he clearly saw that all men were not sufficiently advanced to attain liberation in one earth-life. Thus he instituted the "Middle Path" and acclaimed it to be the safest for the masses. From time immemorial the disseminators of the wisdom religion have been forced to divide the teachings into two sections,—the exoteric and the esoteric. The exoteric, or outer teaching, is best suited for the masses and the inner, or esoteric teaching, is for the "worthy and well-qualified." Following the strict law of the Ancient Wisdom School, Gautama, while instructing his faithful students, said:

"Conscious of the danger in its depth, Brahma,

I would not preach the Norm of Norms to Men."

This statement of the Buddha in its essence is identical with the teachings of the Master Jesus. It is recorded in Matthew, Chap. 7, Verse 6, that the Master said:

"Give not that which is holy unto the dogs. Neither cast ye your pearls before swine, lest they trample them under their feet and turn again and rend you."

It is also recorded that while the Master was conversing with a Canaanitish woman He declared that, "It is not meet to take the children's bread and cast it to the dogs."

Other passages in the four gospels show clearly that the Master spoke to the multitudes in parables, but revealed the true meaning to his faithful followers, and even among his twelve disciples it became necessary for Him to make another division, for did he not take Peter, James and John up into the Mount of Transfiguration? His selection of these three disciples on this momentous occasion clearly shows that of the twelve, only these three were qualified for initiation.

Paul, the Christian Initiate, also guarded the mysteries by giving the rudiments or "milk of the doctrine" to the babes in Christ, but unto those who were worthy and well qualified he revealed the truth. Throughout the ages and in every school of thought a division has been made between the worthy and the unworthy, and the biblical statement that the "Shepherd divideth his sheep from the goats" is well founded. Gautama told his disciples that, "If a Buddha give out occult truths to an unbelieving generation, harm befalls the man who rejects it." It is evident that occult information is withheld from humanity for a twofold reason: First, for the protection of the ignorant who may reject the Truth and therefore suffer the consequences; secondly, to safeguard the Mysteries from those that are developed intellectually, but whose moral qualities are not sufficiently unfolded to prevent them from using the forces of nature for self-aggrandizement, which would also result in self-destruction.

The first sermon which Buddha preached was to a company of five brethern, while he was residing at Benares at Gipatama in the Deer Park. In this discourse the Exalted One outlined the "Middle Path." According to the translation of the Phallic Canon by F. W. Woodward, M.A. (Cantab.), the Enlightened One said:

"Devotion to the pleasures of sense—a low and pagan practice, unworthy, unprofitable, the way of the world (on the one hand), and on the other hand devotion to self-mortification, which is painful, unworthy, unprofitable.

By avoiding these two extremes, He who hath won the Truth (the Buddha) has gained knowledge of the Middle Path which giveth

Vision, which giveth Wisdom, which causeth Calm, Insight, Enlightenment, and Nibbana."

Since crystallization is one of the most potent laws of the physical plane, it is evident that however lofty and idealistic a teaching may be at its inception, it is destined to fall a prey to the mandates which are operating on this mundane plane. From the astrological point of view the planet Saturn is said to govern concretions; his subtle and cold vibrations limit, and obstruct; and as the same planet is designated Regent of India, its crystallizing influence is more evident in that country than elsewhere. It must ever be borne in mind that evolving life can never be held in abeyance on account of man's indolence. Each ego is an integral part of the pulsating stream of life and is responsible for the collective Karma of humanity, as well as suffering the consequences which it has personally generated. The pioneers that are capable of stemming the current shall triumphantly enter the new era on the crest wave of evolution and be given greater opportunities for progress.

In hopes of offsetting the deplorable atheistic state into which the inhabitants of the Western World are fast declining, students of the Ancient Wisdom Teachings have boldly come forward and are endeavoring to reestablish in the hearts of the people the faith and confidence which they once had in the Supreme Ruler of the universe.

Behind these teachers is the energizing power

of a Brotherhood of Adepts who constitute the "Invisible Government," known to all students of occult philosophy. Although the Brothers of this mystic fraternity are unknown to ordinary humanity, they are, nevertheless, potent factors in the polity of every country. Their influence can be traced in the religious organizations of every country. They also lend encouragement to the leaders of material enterprises which are necessary factors in human attainment. Although these great souls are ever active in all the affairs of men, it should be distinctly understood that they influence no one against his will, but willingly encourage and strengthen high ideals wherever found.

Among this august body of adepts are to be found Christian Initiates who are known to students of esoteric Christianity by the name of "Brothers of the Rose Cross." These great souls are more eager to help us, than we are anxious to render assistance to those that are behind us in evolution. In their great desire to help, they utilize the frailest effort we exert in doing good. They recruit students from among the humble and "low-brow," as well as from among the elegant and haughty rich. Thus, if we are truly aspiring to be helpers of humanity we need not be apprehensive because we lack wealth and culture, nor should we be reluctant because we have never acquired a college education. Wealth, culture and learning are indeed helpful, but even though the aspirant possesses all these assets, if he has not unfolded the quality of Love, he may be as the apostle Paul said in First Corinthians, Chapter 13, verse 1: "I am become as sounding brass, or a tinkling cymbal." In the same chapter the apostle also states: "Love never faileth;" and in occult parlance it is stated that: "Even though all other qualities may be undeveloped, yet if the aspirant's heart has been awakened, he shall be able to render invaluable service in the Master's vineyard." In the Masonic legend we also find that the heart-awakening is given precedence over the reasoning faculty. Hence the saying, "The candidate must first be made a Mason in his heart."

It must not be supposed because the heart development plays such an important part in spiritual unfoldment that the aspirant to occult knowledge should neglect his academic training. But since there is danger of over-estimating the "Eye Doctrine," we cannot refrain from making mention of it. Mind alone cannot comprehend the highest. Thus Lao Tze said: "The reason that can be reasoned is not the eternal reason." Occult philosophy aims at helping us to lay hold of that eternal reason—that reason of the heart, which according to Paschal, the "head knows not of."

The Cosmic Christ Principle which manifests as "Love" is primarily rooted in the Sun—the heart of the Grand Man of the Universe. In harmony with the Hermetic axiom "As above, so below," the heart-chakra of the microcosm is the channel through which the "Love Ray" emanates from the Christ within; and when the cardiac chakra is first awakened, it is said by clairvoyants to resemble the fiery disc of the noonday Sun. As the disciple advances on the path of wisdom and love, the rate of vibration of his various centers is accentuated a thousand fold. Thus its color of golden hue changes to indescribable splendor. By loving self-forgetting service, the disciple brings into play the tri-colored serpentine spinal fire, or "Kundalini Sakti" which is the energizing and sustaining force on which every helper of humanity depends. The awakening of this threefold energy is one of the many secrets which are guarded from the undeveloped, but suffice it to say that when one is truly ready to be of service to humanity, he will be entrusted with certain occult instructions which will awaken him to self-consciousness, so that, in an intelligent manner, he can be able to render to all mankind that greater service.

Everyone agrees that LOVE is the great cohesive force in the universe, and when altruistic love is awakened in the humblest of the human family, that soul becomes a radiating center, toward which others are attracted. The awakening of this force transforms the aspirant's whole being; he has, so to say, become a new creature and could never be cold and unsympathetic any more than a stove, in which fire is kindled, could be prevented from radiating heat. Such a person needs no credentials or authorization from organized societies. Charged with the burning fever of altruism, he is received at face value and commands the unsolicited admiration and respect of those whom he contacts. The dwellers of hovels, as well as of palaces, anxiously swing ajar their doors to him; he is hailed as a child of light and love, a true servant of humanity.

Occult parlance states that "Cosmic law works unfailingly for him who works with it." Therefore, if an aspirant, searching for the Truth is not in possession of health, education, or the necessities of material life, these so-called gifts can become his portion, if he is persistent in his quest for Truth. In other words, if the aspirant does abandon his pertinacious qualities, he shall some day acquire full soul quality as well as the mundane things he lacks.

Therefore, when we say "Cosmic law works for him who works with it," we are merely stating in another way the familiar adage, "God helps those that help themselves," and when we contact those blessed with health, wealth and wisdom, or those existing in ignorance, poverty and disease, it is quite evident that the law of alternating cycles has brought to them exactly what they have earned.

In order to instruct nascent humanity how to live in harmony with Nature's law, it was necessary to impart knowledge by simple object lessons. The Israelites, for instance, were given the ordinance "Not to muzzle the ox when it treadeth out the corn." In the Christian teachings the same moral confronts us. It is recorded in the Gospel of St. Matthew, Chapter 10, verses 9-10, that the Master, when sending out His disciples, beholding their lack of faith in "cosmic law," uttered this command: "Provide neither gold, nor silver, nor brass in your purses. Neither scrip for your journey; neither two coats, neither shoes, nor yet staves, for the workman is worthy of his meat." It is also recorded in the Gospel of St. Luke, Chapter 22, verse 35, that when the Master sent out His disciples on their final mission, He asked them: "When I sent you without purse and scrip and shoes, lacked ye anything?" and they said, "Nothing."

An analysis of the Christian teachings will convince us that Christ Jesus endeavored to impress on his followers the necessity of acquiring "faith" and the indispensability of coupling "belief with work." He counseled: "My Father worketh hitherto, and I work." It is evident, the practicing of one of these principles while ignoring the other will never bring true spiritual unfoldment.

The apostle James adhering strictly to the doctrine which the Master had promulgated, gave us the vista in His statement: "But wilt thou know, O vain man, that faith without works is dead?" As a matter of fact, there is no failure for him who couples "Faith with Work." There is a saying among the students of the ancient wisdom-teachings that "He who tries to evade the path of labor, shall be forced to retrace his footsteps." All true spiritual teachers know that "Service" is the shortest and safest way to attain illumination; and thus Gautama Buddha declared, "The Middle Path is the Safest."

The world has never been without a goodly number of warm-hearted persons who are constantly contributing liberally to provide food, raiment and shelter for the poor and needy, but very few indeed are willing to forego their own pleasures and give SELF with alms. Ofttimes indiscriminate giving of alms becomes a curse instead of a blessing; therefore we should endeavor to ascertain if a cause is a worthy one before lending a helping hand. Christ Jesus said, "The poor ye have always with you;" and not until after the people shall have cast out of their consciousness the theological bugaboo which is holding them in bondage, can true material or spiritual progress be expected of them. In other words, humanity will remain in such bondage until, of its own volition, it shall break away from the crystallized traditions which are enslaving the mind, thereby rendering it susceptible to poverty and disease. "And ye shall know the truth, and the truth shall make you free," sayeth Christ Jesus, and it is perfectly clear that the Master was referring to the enslaved mind which manifested in the crystallized dogmas to which the people were adhering.

"Subject to decay are all compounded things,"

were the last words of Gautama Buddha, but it is also true that a knowledge of the soul's pilgrimage will greatly ameliorate all physical agonies. In other words, when one knows from personal experience that the soul is an integral part of God, and that "Before Abraham was I am," such a knowledge gives greater courage and fortitude to withstand the various onslaughts to which flesh is heir.

THERE are a goodly number of people whose mental evolution demands their parting from the unreasonable "worm-of-the-dust" doctrine, and the other erroneous, paganistic tenets which Christian theologians are upholding. The pioneers who have gained freedom from theological dogmas have been inspired to give satisfactory answers to those who are beginning to question the authenticity of the faith into which they were born and, in addition to their throwing light on many veiled passages of holy writ, they are also endeavoring to redeem the millions who are drifting to the consciousness of the infidel. The failure of Doctors of Divinity claiming to be representatives of God, to give reasonable answers to many of the perplexing problems of life, has been the chief cause for the wave of atheism which is now encircling the globe. In other words, humanity is clamoring for the "bread of life," but theology has only a "stone" to offer.

It is the idea of nearly all church-goers that the pioneers of thought who can no longer adhere to the old forms of worship are enemies thereof, and the belief prevails that the innate desire of those who are questioning the soul's pilgrimage, is to overthrow the teachings of Christ Jesus. But contrary to such a belief, these progressive individuals are endeavoring to re-establish the true teachings of the Holy Nazarene. As a matter of fact, by questioning the truthfulness of traditional beliefs, these advanced souls have contacted the radiant light of truth. Tasting a little of the truth, they in turn feel it is their bounden duty to impart to others the knowledge they have acquired, and promulgate the universal religious doctrine which has been taught by Buddha, Jesus, and other great world-teachers.

It is obvious that happiness on this mundane sphere would be greatly enhanced if the minds of humanity were free from the many erroneous, paganistic beliefs which have been disseminated by hierophants of the innumerable sects into which the Christian faith is divided.

The absurd belief that "man is a worm of the dust" and the falsehood that his salvation is solely dependent upon believing in the "cleansing blood of Christ Jesus," are befogging to the mind; the spirits of those who believe such theological concepts are rendered partially helpless in stemming the current of the surging sea of life, and were it not for these erroneous tenets to which the ignorant masses tenaciously adhere, the minds of the youthful generation could readily be moulded to grasp the highest ideals of which the human mind is capable. Future events usually cast their shadows before; hence, those who are qualified to read the signs of the times claim, that there is every reason to believe that the civilization of the aggressive western races will be greatly enhanced when the "Doctrine of Reincarnation" shall have taken the place of the various false beliefs prevalent in the minds of nearly all humanity.

The acceptance of the Doctrine of Rebirth establishes eternal peace between the belligerent head and the sympathetic heart. Step by step the reasoning intellect learns to heed the dictates of this benevolent heart, which in like manner learns not to refute the things which the intellect sanctions.

It is obvious that if a mutual ground is not established between head and heart, human evolution will ever continue to be one-sided, and we shall never attain the rounded development which is so much discussed among the students of sacred wisdom religion.

When the budding mind has once been impressed that reincarnation is a fact and that man is truly an evolving "Deity," it will not be many decades before the whole human family will recognize present conditions, whether good or bad, as results of our past actions and, in like manner, that future happiness will depend solely upon our present mode of living.

It can readily be seen that when the people are convinced that the Doctrine of Reincarnation is not by any means a "fable hatched out of the demented minds of HEATHEN oriental PRIESTS," (for such is the idea which the educators of the western world have impressed upon the minds of the laity), a great change is destined to take place in Christendom and this and many other erroneous beliefs shall have given way to this Doctrine. In it there can be found no excuse by which we may shift our responsibilities to the Creator, or claim that inheritance is the cause of our shortcomings and mental or physical environments.

When the aspirant has been convinced that he is truly an integral part of God, he will realize that his future happiness is solely dependent upon his own merit and such an awakened spirit would deem it an unpardonable sin to ask assistance of others.

With knowledge comes greater responsibility. Therefore, it can readily be seen, how and why the custodians of the SACRED MYSTERIES do not give esoteric instruction, until after the disciple has been "duly and truly prepared, worthy and well qualified" to receive it.

As a matter of fact, when the disciple is awakened to the truth about life and being, and during the struggle for existence, if he should solicit outside help, such an act would recoil, become a barrier, and block the way of progress until he has grown sufficiently strong to stand alone and cope with the disturbing conditions of daily life. Occult investigations have proven that when the aspirant accepts help from without he is "Sinning against the Holy Ghost." In other words, after the disciple has been instructed in the mysteries concerning his divine origin, should he then spurn or reject the indwelling spirit,—ever ready to render assistance and work for his eternal welfare, such weakness is considered AN UNPARDONABLE SIN.

IT SHOULD be evident to even the casual observer that our present system of education is partially responsible for many of our mistakes. As a matter of fact our present modes of acquiring education and culture are the incubators which are hatching the millions of human parasites that are continually scourging humanity. No one who has given a moment's serious thought to the crime-wave which is sweeping the entire world, and which seems to have reached its apex on the American continent, can fail to see that the kind of education now being taught to the youth is partially responsible for the moral status of society.

It cannot be denied that ignorance of cosmic law is the primal cause of all crime and social evil. It is also clearly to be seen that the continued violating of natural laws has been the main cause of poverty, disease, and finally death. The Avatars who have been instructed how to live in harmony with cosmic law have unfolded the "Inner Light," and the acquisition of "Spiritual Insight" has assisted them in the amelioration of a great deal of suffering which they otherwise would have had to endure. These enlightened ones who have drunk of the Fount of Wisdom, have declared that "seeking to know oneself is the only redemption from pain and woe;" thus the adage that "Ignorance is the only sin, and applied knowledge is man's only salvation," is a truism.

It is the belief that progress along spiritual lines is chiefly made by those taking active part in religious orders, and that eternal happiness shall be attained only by the laities, recognized as the main support of the Christian faith. But, contrary to the narrow concepts of orthodox Christians, even the men and women of the business world, although not in the least interested in a future existence, are making rapid spiritual progress; yea, in many instances, they are rendering greater service in the Master's vineyard and developing more soul qualities than those who are pillars of the church. The upright life of many of the so-called heathens and advocates of atheism is sufficient proof to verify the foregoing statement, for when seen in the light of occult science, spirituality does not depend upon the joining of religious organizations; neither do prayers or incantations necessarily foster soul growth. Prayer is helpful if accompanied by labor, but the faithful performance of duty in any direction is the greatest means by which soul growth may be acquired.

"Although your knees are never bent,
  To heaven your hourly prayers are sent;

And be they formed for good or ill,
Are registered and answered still."

The true meaning of the words of Ralph Waldo Emerson quoted above, can readily be recognized in the philosophies of the practical men and women of the world. Although we call them materialists because they are in no wise interested in religious organizations, nevertheless they possess an innate feeling of satisfaction that they are playing indispensable parts in the great plan of evolution. The Latin axiom "Laborare est orare,"—to labor is to worship,—is their motto, and although they have never been convinced of the soul's immortality they innately feel that, if the soul does survive the grave, they have the same opportunity for eternal happiness as those who are daily importuning the THRONE OF GRACE to have mercy upon their souls.

All the successful peoples of the world have agreed that success can be acquired and maintained only by the continued practice of two principles: first by persistently directing their energies in the particular field of service in which they are engaged, and secondly by absolute straight forwardness in dealing with people. It is evident in many instances that these sterling qualities are entirely lacking in those teaching the Doctrine of Soul-Salvation.

A salesman is most successful when he is thoroughly familiar with the method used in producing the goods he offers for sale, and when he is convinced that such articles are of the highest standard.

Since the majority of our so-called Doctors of Divinity are merely professional men who have never been spiritually awakened, they do not possess the reassurance that the SOUL is immortal, and since the Divine Fire has not been kindled within them, they have not the power to kindle it in others. In mystic parlance it is said that "they have no seed to sow." Having never been emancipated from their physical bodies, and having never seen the immortal spirit in man, they are forced to admonish their followers to have faith in the "redeeming blood of Christ Jesus." But the author maintains that the age of blind faith is on the decline, and the people are withdrawing from orthodox Christianity and searching for knowledge from whatever source it may be acquired.

Since our so-called Doctors of Divinity are yet "blind leaders of the blind," it is obvious that the "bread of wisdom," which alone can satisfy the inquiring spirit, can not be supplied by them. The people are clamoring for "bread" but they receive a "stone," and the result is that institutions, which are established on creeds and dogmas are, by degrees, being forsaken for more reasonable beliefs. To offset the gradual decline of patronage, the temples of worship are fast being changed into places of amusement, where ham, turkey and chicken-dinners are being served, and moving-picture entertainments and radio concerts programmed. Whenever spiritual organizations are forced to resort to such means in order to hold the attention of the people, it is most evident that the "sacrificial fire" is burning low, and is therefore badly in need of rekindling.

Recently I was conversing with a group of college students regarding the professions they were about to take up as their life's work. Indeed, these young men were the most promising I have contacted for quite a while. A few of these students had decided to become medical doctors, others dentists, others lawyers or engineers, and still others theologians. Among those who were contemplating the ministry, I discerned the lack of that vital spark which was lighting up the faces of most of their fellow-students. Even a person who has not unfolded spiritual perception could see the glowing of the inner light in the eyes of those who had chosen the material professions as they emphasized their determination to make good in the world's work.

The life-giving energy which was most potent in the other groups was also in evidence in our prospective theologians, but it is regrettable to say that a keen observer could clearly discern among the theological groups, a flickering of the inner light; the young men had begun to assume a false personality to cope with a work for which they had no calling. In an unconscious way they had started to strangle the indwelling Spirit which must ever be the beacon light and driving force of him who succeeds, either in mundane or spiritual pursuits. As a matter of fact, the initiatory degree into all occult schools consists of the awakening of that Indwelling Spirit, and it is obvious that when a school of philosophy teaches its followers to suppress the creative energy instead of accelerating and transmuting it, spiritual illumination and the freedom of the Spirit from its prison house of flesh can never be attained.

Frequent conversations with theological students have convinced me that in nearly all instances the ministry has been entered merely as a profession, and I am thoroughly convinced that the number of those who have been inspired to the holy office for the rendering of self-forgetting service, is indeed very small. Nor does it require the searching eye of a sage to verify such a claim. Whenever mundane duties are engaged in with ulterior motives, the highest good is never achieved, and likewise when the STILL SMALL VOICE has not prompted one to enter the holy office of the priesthood, it is impossible for such an one to acquire wisdom and understanding pertaining to life and being on super-physical planes. Yea, even though the degree of Doctor of Divinity be conferred on such an aspirant, the acquisition of such a degree can in no wise awaken the slumbering indwelling Christos, admittedly the only medium through which man may self-consciously contact the indwelling Spirit, and the primal source of Wisdom.

An intellectual concept of God and the universe, although a great asset to the truth seeker, must not by any means be confounded with "spirituality." An intellectual attainment is but the Doctrine of the Eye, and in occult parlance it is said that unless the Heart Doctrine be blended with the Eye Doctrine, true spiritual illumination can never be attained.

When analysis is made of a person who has attained spiritual illumination, a distinct chemical change of the body is seen to have taken place, and the orthodox sayings, "Born of the Spirit" and "New Birth," are not erroneous claims. Spiritual illumination sets every atom of the body spinning to a higher degree of vibration. Therefore, from an occult point of view that which is usually termed "spiritual illumination" is considered but one of the many phases of spiritual alchemy.

When an aspirant is duly and truly prepared for a spiritual awakening, the physical touch, or mere voice of the adept, is ofttimes sufficiently powerful to awaken in him the slumbering spirit.

The process of awakening or accelerating the vibrations of the candidate may be likened to the changes which take place among the atoms of a piece of steel which are going through the process of magnetization. After accelerating the vibrations of the atoms, the steel will readily attract unto itself iron filings; but even then its cohesive power will be limited to the proportion of magnetism which has been absorbed. Thus according to the law of vibration, if the atomic structure of a spiritual leader has not been vivified by his own awakened spirit, he could no more arouse the slumbering Christ in his followers, than could a piece of unmagnetized steel attract unto itself iron filings.

It can be truly said that the majority of leaders and teachers of religious sects have no knowledge of the fundamental principles of life and being. Yea, many of the hierophants of the Christian teachings are not themselves in possession of absolute faith in the creed which they are promulgating. As a matter of fact, very few educated Christian believe in the "Immaculate Conception" as taught by the various branches of the Christian faith; and surely it is only the most mentally deficient who regard the salvation of men's souls as dependent upon their acceptance of the doctrine of the power of the "cleansing blood of the Lord Jesus Christ."

It cannot be denied that the two theories which have been mentioned concerning the miraculous resurrection of the Lord, are the cornerstones on which exoteric Christianity is established. Anything in which there is a phase of mystery seems to be able to attract the minds of the credulous masses; awe-stricken, they stand and think it an unpardonable sin in him who dares to question its veracity. On the other hand there are a few daring souls who repudiate such beliefs. Among this group are to be found students of the various schools of the ANCIENT WISDOM RELIGION. The latter know that theories, symbols and enigmas are but vestments of the truth, causing them to discard the husks, and eat of the kernel (the manna from heaven), recognized by all as the true wisdom on which the superstructure of all religions is established.

About six hundred years prior to the advent of Christ Jesus, Gautama Buddha advised his followers to "accept nothing that is unreasonable; discard nothing as unreasonable without proper examination." By heeding the warning of the Illuminated One, advanced thinkers and students of comparative religion have discovered that the claims of the clergy of exoteric Christianity are every whit unreasonable; yea, the briefest perusal of religious philosophies is sufficient to convince the earnest student, that fundamentally all religions are the same. The claim that the Christian faith is the only door through which mankind may be saved, is preposterous; and it is but one of the many concoctions which the priesthood has devised to keep the laity in mental slavery. The souls that have evolved sufficiently to cast off the shackles of orthodoxy, have all agreed that self-dependence is a most enviable quality, without which spiritual growth or lasting mundane successes could never be attained. Yet in the Christian faith the aspirant is taught a doctrine to the contrary, namely:—TO BE DEPENDENT. He is advised to throw his every burden on the shoulders of Christ Jesus, since only through Christ Jesus can mankind be saved.

It is evident that, if the Christian races were living in conformity with such a belief, in a few decades a race of spineless weaklings would result. On the other hand, although these same Eastern races have failed to live up to the Doctrine of Buddha, and have likewise failed to tread the "Middle Path" (instituted that egos might enjoy a certain amount of material comfort while developing their potential energies into dynamic powers), they, nevertheless, have remained steadfast in their belief in the "Atma Buddhi,"—the God within,—as the only means of acquiring enlightenment. Everyone who has obtained the slightest glimpse of the truth agrees that man's salvation is solely dependent upon the inner-birth of the Buddha or Christ Consciousness. Hence was the admonition of the initiate Paul, "Until Christ be formed in you."

The self-reliant man of the business world stands out from among his companions. He is the so-called torch bearer, and all who contact him are to some extent benefitted. The most arduous and disagreeable work is usually play for such a one; he radiates life, energy, power and love; he is, indeed, a magnetic center, to contact whom, those that are "weary and heavy-laden" usually receive encouragement to continue in the battle of life. He could not be otherwise, for in him has been awakened the slumbering Christos which has, so to say, made him a new creature. Yea, such an one is ever aglow, and as a stove with ignited carbon could not fail to emit heat, in like manner does a self-dependent man radiate the vibrations of the "Quickened Spirit," which has power to awaken kindred souls to self-consciousness.

On the other hand, when the inner-urge and self-dependence are lacking, the simplest work becomes a burden and failure is necessarily the outcome. How clearly does it appear that to whatsoever faith the spiritual teacher may belong, the quality of self-reliance is an absolute prerequisite; not to be spiritually awakened is the cause for teachers of exoteric Christianity directing their followers unto an exterior saviour—to Jesus, the man,—who has attained union with Christ—identical with the Cosmic Principle which Gautama, the prince of Kapilavastru, had also attained six hundred years B. C. It must ever be remembered that at-one-ment, or union with the Cosmic Christ Principle, is the goal toward which all creation is moving.

It is said that among the early Christians only those that had the spiritual awakening were eligible for the ministry; but conditions have greatly changed, and in these days the ministry is considered a mere profession. Thus spiritual awakening is not considered as necessary; all that is now required is that the candidate declare his belief in the birth, death and resurrection of Christ Jesus; he then acquires a theological education which entitles him to receive credentials from the dignitaries of the chosen denomination, to which he swears allegiance.

It is not my desire to destructively criticize the ministry of Christian orthodoxy, but I cannot refrain from pointing out the shortcomings apparent to everyone, who will give a moment of thought to the religious question. It is my firm belief that if the ministers of the Christian faith had the slightest glimpse of the soul's pilgrimage, they could not deny the "Law of Rebirth" and its concomitant,—the "Law of Consequence."

It can readily be seen that if these cosmic laws were accepted, the established belief that "Jesus is the only begotten Son of God" would at once be ruled out of existence. It is also obvious that the acceptance of these laws would necessitate the revision of the entire superstructure of Christian theology. Thus, although the laws of Rebirth and Consequence were taught by the founder of the Christian faith, there is very little hope that the existing hierophants are going to promulgate any philosophy which is pregnant with ideas that would shatter the superstructure upon which their temporal powers have been established and perpetuated.

As a mark of distinction the existing hierophants of the Christian faith have appropriated unto themselves the title of Doctors of Divinity.

But such titles are ofttimes masks behind which ignorance stealthily lurks. There are but few of these Doctors who are willing to rely on the God within to cure their ills. We can therefore attribute their actions to but one reason and that is, they have not merited spiritual illumination; and since they have not contacted the Christ within, they are, necessarily, unable to give an intelligent explanation for the wiles and woes of suffering humanity.

Our medical men are doing their best to ameliorate human suffering, but since chronic diseases are mental,—or in other words Karmic manifestations of previous thoughts and actions,—pellets and powders have not proven a success in healing the culprits who have been caught in their own nets. Thus with all our numerous scientific discoveries, the halt, the blind, the deaf and poverty-stricken are undoubtedly becoming more numerous. Anyone questioning this statement may satisfy himself by visiting a few of the hospitals and poorhouses in any of our large cities.

Because of the above statements, the author may be dubbed a pessimist; but be that as it may, it is only facts that have been stated and he is not in the least concerned with what the theorists have to say. It is to be expected that the question will arise: "If what has been written is the truth, then is the human race destined to die out by incurable diseases?" My answer to this question is: humanity must continue to suffer until it adjusts itself to the Middle Path. Anyone who endeavors to practice right thought, right speech and right action, will eventually find the panacea for human woes within himself. The God within is the Great Physician, and he who relies on the indwelling Spirit shall be immune from diseases; yea, he "shall run and not be weary; he shall walk and not faint."

THE Master Jesus, when sending out his disciples, admonished them to "heal the sick," but, sad to say, the ministers of the Christian faith have deliberately ignored this most vital aspect of the Christ's teachings. In recent years, aspiring souls outside the pale of the church have discovered that man possesses an indwelling force. In their earnest quest for truth, they received revelations which convinced them that it was upon this INDWELLING SPIRIT that the Master relied. When Jesus sought to replenish His soul, it was to this inexhaustible fount of love, wisdom and power that He fled, and which never failed Him. In an indirect way, He referred to it as "MY FATHER in Heaven"—for did he not say "The Kingdom of Heaven is within you?" Thus this supreme force, which is truly the "FATHER." reigns in this kingdom within. All illumined sages and saints are ever on the alert, ever listening to the "Inner Voice"—which is the "God Within."

The acquisition even to the slightest degree of "Spiritual Sight with Insight," is sufficient to convince the aspirant that the "Crucifixion of the Christ" was in reality not a momentary occurrence which happened nearly two thousand years ago to one individual on Mt. Calvary, but a demonstrated fact to every aspirant who has attained illumination. At this stage of the aspirant's unfoldment, he will discover that Christ is not a person but is, instead, a "Cosmic Principle" which is being crucified daily in all the kingdoms of Nature.

The occult-scientist acknowledges Christ as a universal Principle, and those who have unfolded the clairvoyant sight behold in every atom the Christ or Buddhic Principle, as a radiating center of force; on the other hand, his spiritual insight reveals to him that action is the fanning process. Therefore through aeons of activity, the divine monad, which is a part of the Christ Principle, and which forms the centrosome of the atom, develops into a dynamic God.

Like human beings, some atoms are further along on the path of attainment than others; in other words, some are more charged with the vital essence of life.

The law governing the "Force of Attraction and Repulsion" is well known to material science, and gives rise to the saying that "atoms love and hate." By the application of the law numerous useful ingredients have been compounded by the wizards of chemistry. For example: Oxygen and hydrogen are component parts of water, but if we throw sodium into it we shall find that there is a close affinity between this sodium and the oxygen, whereby they readily unite and form another compound called "Sodium Hydroxide," very different from the former, and the escaping hydrogen may be collected. In fact, many of the various gases are produced by this method.

Since atoms love and hate, it is logical to concede that unto the atomic sphere must we go to find the primal cause for both the sympathy and antipathy, which are most apparent in human beings. The atoms which compose the bodies of the Negro race are vibrating at a different rate from those which compose the bodies of the Anglo-Saxon races, and it is the clash of vibrations which causes the existing inharmony among peoples, sects and individuals.

The spiritual Alchemist can discern by clairvoyance or by Star Chemistry, whether a man and woman entering wedlock are united harmoniously or otherwise. In the near future, material scientists may also be able to discern, through analysis of the blood, if peace and concord will prevail between those who are entering holy matrimony.

Since we are but finite beings, our knowledge of astrology, clairvoyance and chemical analysis may fail us; but there is one thing which the initiate Paul declared NEVER FAILETH, and that is "LOVE." Thus in occult parlance it is said that, "When the love aspect of the Triune Spirit is awakened, such an aspirant is in constant touch with Cosmic Wisdom;" the Christ or Unifying Principle of the Cosmos has been born within, the magic touch of which sets every atom of the aspirant's body aglow; he has, so to say, reached at-one-ment, and can vibrate in peace, love and concord with all men. Hence it is said that:

"He who sees the truth, is neither of the East
   Nor of the West—He is of God."

Those who have attained illumination are cognizant that all religions are bound together with the golden thread of truth; they see in all kingdoms the ONE LIFE of the Logos which enables them to look to the "God Within" for redemption, and not to the personal Christ who died on Golgotha. In other words, the white light of truth has freed them from the bondage of creed, race and country, and, like Tom Paine, they can triumphantly chant the psalm of freedom: "The world is my country, and to do good is my religion."

By persistent effort they have discovered the KEY whereby the door of the prison-house of flesh may be opened, and by their own volition free the mind and astral vehicles from this prison-house. The Greek sage Empedocles referred to this "self-conscious state" in the following words:

"When leaving the body behind thee, thou
   soarest into the ether,
There thou becomest a God, immortal, not
   subject to death."

Had the laity been instructed in the most rudimentary lessons of the Ancient Wisdom Teachings they could never have been so willing to accept the various unreasonable creeds which are year by year becoming more numerous. The mere acceptance of occult teachings is usually of sufficient importance to convince the aspirant that man is a "God in the making" and consequently a potential Diety.

Unless one is mentally deficient, he cannot fail to grasp the reasonable hypotheses that are set forth throughout the entire "Doctrine of Rebirth." Only the mentally undeveloped can fail to conceive that such tenets as the "Immaculate Conception" or the "Saving Power of the Blood of Christ Jesus," or the "Reunion of Soul and Body on the final Resurrection Morn," are but so many allegories which have been instituted by the early priesthood for the purpose of veiling the Sacred Mysteries from the comprehension of the unworthy masses.

And, sad to say, the motives of the early hierophants were pregnant with the deadly germ of SELFISHNESS. Crystallization did, as a result, set in and the ministers of the Gospel, unable to uncover the hidden meanings which are contained in the various allegories, are teaching the mere "letter of the law."

The constant repetition of these myths has caused a phase of self-hypnosis, and many of the learned Doctors of Divinity believe that these fables are unadulterated truths handed down to man by the Creator. It is therefore obvious that the custodians have lost the key to the Sacred

Mysteries, and the "blind are leading the blind." "Oh, let not the flame die out! Cherished age after age in the dark caverns, in its holy temples cherished. Fed by pure ministers of love: Let not the flame die out!"

These words of Edward Carpenter are pregnant with courage and vital energy and he who has been spiritually awakened can readily see that even in this so-called "deplorable materialistic age" the "FLAME" is still being fed by "true ministers of love." Few may be the messengers but, nevertheless, they usually are sufficiently spiritualized to rekindle this dim, quivering flame with the oil of gladness.

Through the inspired and convincing lectures of the disciples of the Masters of the Wisdom, a great number of people are yearly being converted to the belief of "Rebirth," and the terror-stricken effect of believing in the "Hell-Fire Doctrine" is fast waning; vast numbers are convinced that a final resurrection morn, when soul and body shall be reunited, is but another paganistic myth concocted by the crafty priesthood to keep the people in ignorance and fear. Those that have been liberated from the errors of pagan belief, and who claim that the soul and body on a final day of judgment are to be reunited, have resorted to cremation as a more rational and sanitary method for disposing of the dead. It is hoped that, in the near future, the millions of dollars which are being spent yearly for expensive caskets, flowers,

THE MIDDLE PATH 75

tombstones, the upkeep of cemeteries, and the numerous other nonessentials lavished on the dead, will be spent more constructively to help those toiling on in the flesh. When a few such changes are made in crystallized orthodox Christianity, the day when "Thy will be done on earth as it is in heaven" will have been hastened.

Every one who has given a moment's serious thought to the spiritual side of life is convinced that health, wealth, and all the things contributing to our mundane enjoyment, are but crude reflections of the spiritual joy and felicity which are in store for us. We cannot deny that at a certain stage of our unfoldment, possessions do add to bodily comfort and enjoyment; neither can we deny that health and wealth require wisdom and understanding to give lasting happiness, without which they ofttimes prove to be curses instead of blessings.

It is most evident that if complete happiness could be attained during mundane existence, very little progress would be made. Nature has implanted in every living creature the germ of discontent, for dissatisfaction alone will inspire us to achieve these greater heights and glories which are beyond the concepts of finite mind. Yea, even among the celestial hosts there is ever present the divine discontent which urges them onward from one plane of glory to another; there is ever present that hunger and thirst to discover the MYSTERIOUS UNKNOWN—a veritable striving to become ONE with the primal source of existence. "Happy is he who has seen the mysteries, and then descends under the hollow earth. He knows the end of life; and he knows the beginning promised by Zeus."

These words of Pindar should give encouragement to those seeking to uncover the mysteries; but let him who enters the stream pay strict heed to the warning words of Buddha, that his footsteps may not stray from the "Middle Path," for this is beyond all doubt the safest:

"Not nakedness, nor matted hair, nor filth,
Not fasting long, nor lying on the ground,
Not dust and dirt, nor squatting on the heels,
Can cleanse the mortal that is full of doubt.
But one that lives a calm and tranquil life,
Though gaily decked,—if tamed, restrained he live,
Walking the holy path in righteousness,
Laying aside all harm to living things,—
True mendicant, Ascetic Brāhmin he."

End of Part Two.

PART THREE

The pages that follow, constituting Part Three of this volume are taken from the author's book, "Steps to Self-Mastery," and are reproduced here because they so completely emphasize the wisdom of "Following the Middle Path."

Since the purpose of this work is to impress upon and convince the reader that to "follow the Middle Path" is not only "The Safest" but also the SUREST way to eternal happiness, it was thought timely to again call public attention to the sentiments expressed in that former publication.

THE pupils of all occult schools, whether Eastern or Western, are divided into three grades: students, probationers, and disciples. The student is one who has become interested in some occult philosophy and desires to make a start upon the Path. Often, perhaps usually, his motive is at first selfish; he feels that he has outgrown the worldly life and wishes to attain for himself knowledge and virtue. However, even this is constructive. As Mephisto enigmatically described himself to Faust as "part of that power which still produceth good, whilst ever scheming ill," so the student is better employed in the pursuit of the higher knowledge, though he work for self alone, than in spending his time in gossip, frivolous amusements, or the reading of trashy literature. As he begins to advance upon the Path, his motive will be gradually purified, and he will know that in order to raise himself he must lift also the Self of all mankind.

In ancient Egypt, Syria, and Chaldea, religion, art, and science were taught as one, and in the true occult schools of India and America they are so considered to this day. However, the Elder Brothers of evolution, who constitute what may be termed a species of invisible government, have seen fit to divorce these branches for a time in the Western World with the apparent object of developing that concentrated "one-pointedness," which seems to be the special quality of our modern civilization, but these three are one, and their essential unity will appear once more upon the surface before the close of this cycle. By this temporary process of separation mankind is obtaining the quintessence of each, and upon the next loop of the spiral, will be able to blend them again in a higher and more harmonious whole.

Religion, art, and science are a veritable trinity, the equilateral triangle which has always been used as the symbol of the Divine. The ego upon the path of evolution must pass through each of these in turn, and when it reaches the point where it has attained to a certain degree of proficiency in each—has built the triangle within itself—it may begin to extract from these experiences that quintessence which constitutes the threefold soul of man. We should ever remember that immortality is yet to be won, and it is only by the building of the soul—the vehicle of immortal self-consciousness—that this may be accomplished. In the great majority of people the triangle is not yet equilateral, and every individual will be directed by his own ego to that school where he may best obtain those experiences needed for his development, and receive the assistance of a Master to whom he is sympathetically attuned. For example, if the triangle be deficient upon the side of the conscious soul, he will be impelled to labor in the material world, where the physical impacts received will have their effects in the higher realms and assist to develop that aspect of the triangle which is lacking. His particular line of work will be determined by his individual evolution, and may range from hard manual toil to the esthetic labors of the sculptor or artist. If he be alert, and learn his lesson before the end of his present embodiment, he may leave that condition and enter into another, where he may work upon a different aspect of the triune soul. However, if he is well polarized, and desires to remain in his vocation, he may proceed to develop the emotional soul by the practice of religion, and the intellectual soul by the study of science, making no outward change whatever, and rendering selfless service to humanity just where he is. We should be careful never to judge a man's spiritual condition by his physical body, environment, or intellectual development. A Chinese coolie, belonging to the seventh Atlantean sub-race, if he adheres to the Middle Path and has succeeded in the development of the equilateral triangle of the soul, will be nearer to the goal of self-consciousness, and during his after-death state will have more enjoyment of the Heaven he has created, than a modern Anglo-Saxon with a string of college degrees whose development is not in equilibrium.

The law of crystallization is ever dominant upon the physical plane, and the high ideals which we endeavor to bring into objective existence becomes hardened in their descent, and we find too often that we have for our pains only the letter which killeth. The threefold school of Religion, Art, and Science was inaugurated by the Masters of Wisdom for the benefit of humanity, but in the mad rush of the age it has become so deplorably crystallized that only a few of the spiritually awakened are able to visualize its original purity of purpose. The pioneers of the human race have now passed their involutionary stage, and are entering upon the ascending arc; therefore the custodians of the Lesser Mysteries, our Elder Brothers, are now endeavoring to reunite the three branches of knowledge, by showing to the world that science embraces both art and religion, that art in its higher aspects is both religious and scientific, and that religion in the beauty of its aspirations and achievements and the unvarying exactness of its principles fundamentally comprises both art and science. Aspirants who have become conscious of the underlying unity of these three schools, know also that they are but doors to experience, by means of which man is slowly evolving to his appointed end—the immortal and self-conscious Creator.

The step from student to probationer is not an easy one; it involves certain inevitable inharmonies—mental, physical, and spiritual—and happy is the ego who is able to rise above them. The first and most essential duty of the new probationer is to change the atomic structure of the body, thus making it a better instrument for the use of the spirit. This is not an easy task, and the student must go about it intelligently, otherwise mental and physical torture and an early grave may be the result. There are many ways of making this change, including fasting and various systems of diet, such as fruit and nuts, raw vegetables, etc., but after considerable investigation I have resorted to the old method of allowing the body to choose for itself, or perhaps not precisely the body, but the spiritual essence which is encased in every cell—we may call it the cell soul.

By the law of chemical change a substance

without ceasing to exist may be changed into one which is new and entirely different. In combining two or more substances in a chemical compound, the experimenter has no choice as to what proportions of the substances he will use—the proportion is determined by the nature of the substances themselves. Thus in the formation of iron rust or ferric oxide, iron will combine with oxygen in the proportion of one hundred parts iron to forty-three parts oxygen—no more, no less. In like manner, by the law of elective affinity, the cells of the body select certain foods by which to rebuild their own substance, and when we have reached to the stage of probationership, if we pay attention to their prompting, we may rest assured that they will choose exactly those substances which are most necessary for their health, strength, and happiness.

Under these conditions there will be little necessity for the study of vitamines or the wearisome counting of calories, for the appetite will be a certain indication of the food substances which are needed for the rebuilding of the body. However, it must not be supposed that we are to ignore entirely the various systems of dietetics worked out with such pains by our modern food specialists. They are often of great help to the young probationer, and are invaluable to the animal man whose body is poisoned by wrong living, and whose atomic structure, by the same law of elective affinity, still calls for tobacco, pork chops, beer, whiskey, etc. It is clearly to be seen that the system of selecting foods by intuition cannot be recommended to the man of the world; it is for those only whose evolution has brought them to the stage of probationership when they are ready by occult chemistry to consciously rebuild the body.

The word probation implies that one is on trial; it is a state designed to test one's character and qualifications and no one who enters the path of occultism can escape the test. The work of changing the body is truly the touchstone of success in probationership, and it is a most vital factor in the occult life. To accomplish it, two things are necessary: first, right thinking; second, an evenly balanced vegetarian diet. If the aspirant abstains from flesh food, not selfishly, but out of love for his younger brothers of the animal world, and leads a pure life in other respects, not because health or even spiritual development require it, but because his higher self revolts against the life of the senses, he will in time emerge a new creature possessed of a strong and healthy body and a powerful spiritual will by which he is able to bring into subjection all the passions and desires of the lower self.

It is a truth known to all occultists that it is only by the power of the great creative energy that man is able to propel himself into the invisible worlds or to contact his higher self. In order to attain to regeneration the aspirant must conserve this force by a pure life, harness it and set it to work.

In Genesis 2:10-15 reference is made to a river which flows out of Eden and branches into four streams. This is not intended to be taken literally, and it may be said that Eden here symbolizes the physical body with the water of life flowing upward to open for him the gates of the invisible world. We are told that the name of the first stream is Pison, which waters the country of Havilah (the head), where there is much fine gold (the pons), and bdellium and onyx stones (the pituitary body and pineal gland). The second is Gihon, which compasseth about the land of Ethiopia (the solar plexus), and the third is Hiddekel, which goeth eastward to Assyria (the tongue, wherewith we bless or curse). The fourth is Euphrates, which symbolizes that branch of the stream which flows to the organs of procreation.

Every probationer of a true occult school is taught that the creative energy is sacred, and that its conservation is an absolute necessity if he desires to live the higher life. It is my belief that no one can harness this force and direct it in the right way unless he rebuilds his body by means of a vegetarian diet. Why should we infer that the commandment, "Thou shalt not kill," refers to the killing of man alone? For the probationer at least, it includes also the animal kingdom, our younger brothers upon the path of evolution, and he cannot hope to reach discipleship as long as he

THE MIDDLE PATH

continues to feed his body upon their decaying carcasses. By the assimilation of this impure food he assumes something of the nature of this lower kingdom, and somewhere along the path he will be conquered by the purely animal expression of sex, which must inevitably have its outlet. When the probationer succeeds in harnessing the waters of Eden, and is able to direct the full stream of "Pison" to "the country of Havilah," he may begin in earnest to seek out the wisdom of the ages; he is then ready for discipleship, where greater temptations will assail him.

Before he can enter into this new degree, years of preparation are usually required. Often it brings with it the unfoldment of one or more aspects of the sixth sense, such as clairvoyance, clairaudience, etc., and he realizes that he must deal with the finer forces of nature, which have now become apparent to his higher senses, arrayed in pitched battle against him. If he has not entered upon the Path with a selfless motive—if his body is not clean, his heart pure—he will be defenseless against them. To protect himself against their assaults, he must wear the impregnable armor of love and spiritual will, for he is surrounded on all sides, having no avenue of escape except a challenge.

It should not be supposed that students of occultism are using their imagination when they describe to us these hidden forces of nature. All natural phenomena are the result of their operations. They are the upbuilding and disintegrating forces of the Cosmos; without them there would be no vegetation, fire, or winds; neither would there be earthquakes, or volcanic eruptions which are necessary phenomena, for there must be occasional alterations of the surface of the earth to keep pace with changing conditions. To the trained clairvoyant these forces are as real as the massive structures of a city; actually they are far more real, because if directed by the powerful mind of an adept, they could destroy the physical structures of such a city in the twinkling of an eye.

There is not the least doubt that these mysteries were known to the ancients and used as late as the Mosaic dispensation. All the religions of the world are pregnant with them; in Masonry the Craftsman is admonished to search out the hidden forces of nature—but alas, how few are willing to make the effort necessary for spiritual unfoldment. Modern society scoffs at the Mysteries, and he who lives the selfless life and penetrates their secrets is dubbed a spiritualist and a fakir. That greatest of all occult books, the Bible, tells us that we are fighting not against flesh and blood, but principalities and powers of the air. All mankind is battling desperately against unseen forces; the only difference between the average man and the disciple is that the latter by a life of labor has earned the right to behold them face to face.

It is clearly to be seen that one must have

years of occult training before his admission to discipleship; if he be not well balanced mentally, morally, and spiritually before he consciously contacts these hitherto unseen beings, he will surely be deluded and swept off his feet by borderland spirits and various other hierarchies of subhuman entities who are ever ready to serve him—for a price. Should he be in financial straits or selfishly desire wealth or personal aggrandizement, some of these beings may offer to assist him, but woe to him if he ignorantly accepts their help, for he must surely suffer the consequences. According to the law of compensation, if they serve him here, he must serve them on their plane of being, after his earthly life is ended—and often his life of servitude begins while he is still in the body, for these beings miss no single opportunity to entrap the unwary one who foolishly asks their assistance.

In the Bible we read of these forces of nature personified by theology as Satan, the prince of devils, who destroyed the worldly goods of Job by wind and fire, and caused his body to be afflicted with boils. It was these entities also who tempted the Master Jesus, and had he failed to pass the test, he would not have reached to the exalted degree of Christhood. The temptation of these two does not appear strange to students of occultism. They are battling daily with the same forces of nature, and they know that such is the path which every initiate must tread—and not the initiate alone but every other man before he attains to higher knowledge—and thrice happy is he who is able to meet and pass the test.

While lecturing upon this subject, I have several times been asked: "Why is it necessary for one to pass these severe tests before he attains to knowledge?" To answer this question let us resort to the analogy of every day experience. We should ever bear in mind that we are but children in the school of life. In our very youthful days we were sent to kindergarten. After we had advanced beyond the picture book stage, we attended higher and higher classes, where harder and still harder lessons were given, until we reached the age of specialization for our work in life. At this stage a final examination was given to test our qualifications; if we failed, possibly we were forced to take positions we were later ashamed of; if we passed, we were proud of our achievements, and launched out upon the sea of life with great expectations of success—but even then, the testing was not over. If we became self-satisfied, and ceased to feed the mind with new ideas, we quickly retrograded, and in a few short years. those whom we had formerly surpassed forged ahead and left us behind in the race. The sufferings encountered on the Path are the examinations given by the Masters to test our courage—to try our purity of heart—and if we pass, they know that we are ready to go on to higher things.

Although the man who travels the spiral path

advances more slowly than he who treads the way of initiation, his goal is the same. He must have his incentives to action, must battle with the forces of nature, and meet and pass his tests. He may give the life blood of his youth to the pursuit of evanescent shadows, the glitter of gold, and the lure of social prestige, nevertheless we should not condemn him, or try to discourage him if he be inclined to this line of action, for this also is good. Mankind is yet in its infancy, is still in the kindergarten, and if its picture book were taken away, it would have no way of acquiring knowledge—nothing to spur it on to action—and by a slight use of the imagination we may picture the result.

The knights of medieval times, many of them true mystics, were bound by an obligation to unsheathe the sword only in the defense of innocent maidens, destitute orphans, and the religions to which they adhered. Inspired by the inner urge to protect the weak, they performed many valiant deeds.

The youth of that age, inspired by the spirit of chivalry, looked forward to knighthood as their goal; today, the standard has changed and wealth and honor are the end and aim of our existence. Nevertheless, the young man of today has the same spirit of "do or die"; he is battling with nature, and having conquered the elements of earth, water, and fire, is well on his way to the conquest of the air. By the law of alternating cycles we are entering now upon a higher loop of the spiral, and shall recapitulate the age of chivalry. We aspire today to assume the holy obligation of the Knights of the Rose Cross; having discarded our armor of steel we are protected by the shield and buckler of moral courage and a strong, determined will; having laid down the spear and battle axe our only weapon is universal love. Thus, we need not the outer stimuli of wealth and fame, for love itself, symbolized by the pure white rose in the center of the cross, shall be our incentive. As we lave in this living fire of all-inclusive love, the petty distinctions of race and clan shall be burned away, and we shall serve humanity without thought of self, working ever for the Brotherhood of Man.

Only by self-forgetting service can we hope to attain the knowledge of the ages and learn to wield that potent force, greater than electricity or steam, which shall be entrusted to the men of the coming race—a force which can be harnessed only in the human body, prepared and made clean by right living, and directed only by the impulse of the developed will.

The hardships, trials, and tribulations which beset the path of every disciple who challenges the potent and secret forces of nature are absolutely necessary to awaken and test his will. If he be sincere in his quest for knowledge, he will attain; if he enter upon the Path with a selfish motive, he will fail. Knowledge of things spiritual comes only as the crowning glory of a well spent life; it may be attained only by the acme of virtue. The Path is not strewn with roses, but thereon only can immortality be won—there is no other way.

THERE is a growing number of people who in recent years have become dissatisfied with the present order and are looking to philosophy for a solution of their difficulties. Many of the innocent minded ones have given up active work in the world where they were rendering good service to humanity and sought retreat in the arms of some cult, believing that in a few months or years the leaders of said cult would usher them into the empyrean, away from earth and its complicated problems. But alas, how sadly disappointed are the majority of these people. If they enter a true spiritual school, where development is based on the natural law of unfoldment, it is too slow for them. They want quick results, and when the intricate, unavoidable material problems confront them as of yore, they become dissatisfied with the leaders and the society, labeling them materialists and fakers because they themselves have had a wrong conception of spirituality.

The "Middle Path" may be entered wherever we are placed in life, and greater spiritual progress may be made in mending old shoes in a great city, as did the famous mystic, Jacob Boehme, than in going into a retreat and spending all one's time in reading philosophy and meditating on some supposedly high spiritual ideal. Many who join these cults, believing themselves to be extremely liberal, are in reality narrow, conceiving that the society to which they belong is the only one which is conducted under the auspices of the Elder Brothers. Such biased thinking contains the germ of disintegration, and is not far removed from the theological dogma of the laying on of hands.

The Brothers of the Cross are not limited in their activities. They work with all religious movements, and even in the materiality of business life they inspire religious-minded men to work selflessly for the good of humanity. Let us take for illustration a white shaft of light directed to our solar system from the Central Sun. The white light is a synthesis of all the colors of the spectrum. These colors are in reality spiritual pulsations from the white light of the Logos, which must first be neutralized by the planets, or Seven Spirits before the Throne, before it can be used by the seven churches, or schools of the Lesser Mysteries. These Planetary Genii are also distributors of the seven liberal arts and sciences, bestowing upon nations as well as individuals what they have stored up in Nature's lock box until the time of harvesting. Is it not logical to concede that since these Planetary Spirits work through the different churches and Mystery Schools, through nations and individuals, that the White Light—the Path of Attainment—may be entered by any of these portals, wherever we may be? Nations, as well as individuals, must do their best in working with their own Ray, until by the slow process of evolution, or individual unfoldment, the higher vehicles may be spiritualized to withstand the tremendous vibrations of the all-inclusive White Light.

When the White Ray has been attracted, it will awaken the sleeping Logos within, accelerate the sixth sense—that of Intuition— and put man in conscious touch with the forces of Nature, thereby establishing his communion with the Gods.

Mankind is divided into two great classes: those who are still unconscious—held fast in the bonds of matter—and those in whom the spirit is beginning to awaken. To the observing eye of the philosopher, the materialist is on the path of attainment just as much as his more spiritual brother; he, however, is working unconsciously, blinded for the time being by the desire for wealth, fame, and honor. It is a pitiable thing that these ephemeral things must be used to prod us on, but to the young mind they are necessary stimuli. It cannot see beyond form to contact the life within, therefore the objects of the world of form must be used to encourage it. But the time is approaching when these external stimuli will not be necessary, for each will have evolved to the point where he will do his work as a duty, without thought of worldly compensation.

That such an age is approaching no one who has given any time to spiritual thinking will deny. The features of the Coming Race are casting their shadows on those who are to be its forebears, and the things which are now dreams shall be established principles in the new dispensation. But that dispensation is yet far away.

Our young men and women coming out of college filled with life and energy are driving into business for all it is worth. They are drawn into occupations whose rewards are money and fame, flocking to such vocations like moths to a flame, because there they may give free rein to passion and desire. We see them giving their lives on the field of battle or in the air, always engaged in some occupation where youth and red blood are required to materialize schemes for worldly advancement. Upon this path wealth, fame, amusement, and companionship are strewn before their feet. The majority set out with noble ideals, but after a little while their eyes are blinded by that jack-o'lantern of the world—the light of fame—and when the time has arrived for them to return whence they came, they know nothing of the existence beyond. The grave appears to them as an eternal pit—not the beginning of life—but its end. Some having met with trials and hardships and apparent failure, and being ignorant of the laws of rebirth and consequence, have themselves terminated their lives upon this plane. Had these souls been educated in spiritual as well as material things, such tragedies could have been prevented. The spiritual knowledge could then have worked in conjunction with the material, and these unfortunate ones could have rendered much service to humanity.

If we were willing to spiritualize our vocations, we could do more for Christianity in a few decades than theology has done in two thousand years. Actors and actresses could reach thousands daily; the salesmen in the shops, the servants in the homes—all could render service like true artisans, using profession and position not for selfish aggrandizement but for service to mankind. But, alas, how few are willing to enter upon this positive path—the path of service—where morality and chastity are the passports, and trials and tribulations are upon every hand; where the aspirant meets with no words of encouragement from family or friends, and where starvation often stares him in the face until he has learned to live by faith and become a partaker of his Father's bounty.

I call this the positive path, because upon it there are no outside stimuli; the candidate depends solely upon the inner voice. Sometimes he becomes weary and tired of life, but always in the Garden of Gethsemane the White Light shines, and sometimes there is a radiant face, and a voice which says, "Go on!" This is not the false light of the world, but the White Light of the Solar Logos, which shines only for aspiring souls whose crosses have become so heavy that their sweat is like blood and their agony seems too great to be borne. There are a few such souls in the world;

it is they to whom the Bible refers as the salt of the earth, and their number is yearly increasing. They are not striving for social distinction. When forced into positions of leadership they may be known by their simplicity—but of their own choice, they serve always in secret.

One can readily see that it takes a determined soul to travel this spiritual path. It is diametrically opposed to the materialistic tendency of the age; only the advanced soul dares enter it, for he must walk by the true Light and repudiate the false light of Lucifer. It is easy to die at once for a principle, to perform glorious deeds on the field of battle amid the roaring of cannon and the shouts of heroes; but to fight the good fight—to die daily to the desires of the flesh—these things mean a harder battle. To accomplish them requires great fortitude, and absolute mastery of self.

Too much emphasis cannot be placed on the spiritual side of practical things. Our daily work must be done as unto the Lord. The sooner our young men and women learn to spiritualize their daily lives in the business world, that much sooner will health, comfort, and happiness surround them in the vocations which they have selected as their special ways of attainment. The office and the shop will then be places, not of drudgery, but of worship, for "Laborare est orare"—to work is to worship.

There are a few large business organizations

which practice spirituality in dealing with employees. They began by shortening the hours of labor and paying a living wage; by assuming that those who labor are not machines, but men. At once they received a response from both trade and employees; it could not be otherwise, for they put themselves in line with cosmic law. They gave—and in accordance with the law of compensation they are receiving their return. These leaders of industry who are endeavoring to follow the Middle Path are pioneers in the field of human brotherhood, and their new and revolutionary ideas are phsychological harbingers of the coming age.

The key to the narrow way of attainment has not been given to any special individual or to any particular society. It makes no difference how ancient is the claim of the school or the church. According to cosmic law the sun shines on the unjust as well as the just, and in like manner are the operations of the Leaders of evolution. The Master Christ saw fit to choose fishermen to be His helpers, and these souls are still with us in spirit, striving to bring about the ideal of the Christian religion—the union of all creeds, all races, all religions, the resolving of many into one.

Some time ago I attended a lecture given by an Eastern sage—an ascetic of the Sufi. This reverend gentleman was a scholar and master of several languages, but his delivery was so simple a child could understand him. He expounded the six great scriptures of the world, emphasizing the fact that in essence all religions are one, and though not a Christian he manifested the spirit of Christ in every word and action.

In contrast to this gentleman was another who lectured a few days later. He was a member of the Anglo-Saxon race and represented a Christian denomination, yet after impressing upon his audience that the study of certain sciences was essential to spiritual development, he alluded to the people of the East as inferior in development to those of the West, conveying the idea of the great superiority of his own race and culture.

I am a student of comparative religion and a disciple of Western Masters, but I can see no fundamental difference between the teachings of the Masters of the East and the West. When such bigotry is encountered, it should not be attributed to the Great Ones who are working behind the scenes, not for any sect, creed, or order, but for humanity.

As one of the World Saviors, Christ Jesus came to do away with race religion; we, who claim to represent His Holy Order, should cease to emphasize differences and work in harmony with the brothers of the East, North, or South. They also are travelers upon the Narrow Way of Attainment. Until we are able to meet them all on the broad platform of universal tolerance and sympathy, without thought of racial or religious superiority, we are unworthy the name of Christian.

We are all on the path of attainment, whether consciously or not. Perfection is the end and aim of all creation, and the path to that far distant goal is the faithful, every day performance of duty. Our work and our possessions are not gifts to us. Under the slow grinding of the mill of evolution we have progressed to the place where we have merited these things. We have earned them, and by the just law of compensation we have received them. If we continue to be faithful in little things, greater avenues of usefulness shall be opened to us in the future. If we use our professions and our worldly goods as means of doing good, we are storing up greater blessings for future lives on earth. On the other hand, if we use these things for selfish purposes only, in the future we may still possess wealth but no pleasure or happiness will be derived from it because we have given no happiness to others. Truly does the Bible say, "Charity covereth a multitude of sins," although indiscriminate giving may be a curse instead of a blessing, and judgment should be used in this as in all other things.

The great gift to the world is the gift of one's self—a living sacrifice on the altar of service. According to the law of eternal progression which we call evolution, all things are unfolding, though it may be imperceptible to finite minds. Therefore even those who have given all their time and energy to the amassing of wealth for worldly pleasure and aggrandizement of self have made some spiritual progress. But we find that at the end of their lives these souls are never satisfied. The false light of Lucifer, which has been their guiding star, begins to flicker at the approach of trouble, and when sickness befalls them and the men of science can render no help, the light withdraws altogether and the soul is left in spiritual darkness to lament the past.

The last days of those who have lived the spiritual life are always most joyful; the Light which has gone before them shines brighter as the sands of life run low. At the hour meditation, the infant Logos within leaps for joy; every atom of the body is aglow, and pulsates with Cosmic Light. The grave to such souls is not an eternal pit of darkness, but a jeweled casket into which to cast the body, which has served its purpose as the dwelling place of the infant Christ. We are told in the Bible that "the righteous shall not see death." To realize the truth of this statement, we must live the life. If we do this, we shall know by that most convincing of all demonstrations—personal experience.

PART FOUR

IN THE preceding pages a synopsis of Gautama's early childhood is given. We also took into consideration his struggles in severing parental and conjugal ties, as well as his final attainment to enlightenment, and after enlightenment, his apprehensiveness in teaching the "Norm of Norms" to the multitude. We also have briefly considered the similarity of his teaching with that of Jesus, the Christ, and his admonition to those that were striving for illumination "To follow The Middle Path."

That both Gautama Buddha and Christ Jesus gave out only fragments of truth can clearly be discerned in their discourses to their faithful followers.

In St. John's Gospel, sixteenth chapter, twelfth verse, it is recorded that the Master, while discoursing with his disciples, said: "I have yet many things to say unto you, but ye cannot bear them now." And in Buddhic literature it is also recorded that while the Venerable One was residing at Kosambi in a Sinsapa forest, the Wise One took up a few Sinsapa leaves in his hand and said to his disciples: "What do you think, O Monks, which is more, these few Sinsapa leaves I hold in my hands, or the other leaves in the Sinsapa wood above?"—"The few leaves, Lord, that the Venerable One holds in his hands, are small in number; much more are the leaves in the Sinsapa forest above."—"Even so, O Monks, what I have perceived and HAVE NOT communicated to you is much more than what I HAVE communicated to you. And why, O Monks, have I NOT revealed this to you? Because, O Monks, it would NOT be of advantage to you, because it does NOT promote the higher life in all its purity; because it does NOT lead to disgust with the world, to annihilation of all lust, to the ceasing of the transitory, to peace, to the higher knowledge, to awakening to Nirvāna. Therefore, I have NOT communicated it to you. And what, Monks, HAVE I communicated to you; and what the path that leads to the ceasing of suffering, Monks, I HAVE communicated to you."

The histories of all the world's religions show clearly that great Teachers gave out only fragments of truth, from the fount of Wisdom they possessed. It must not be supposed that it was selfishness which caused them to withhold their knowledge. As a matter of fact, they would have been glad to have unburdened themselves of their spiritual treasures, but how could they have done so, when the very rudiments of the truth they gave out were not accepted? In other words, humanity as a whole was not "worthy and well-qualified" to receive these doctrines purposely withheld.

Statements are made throughout the Ancient Wisdom Teachings that, whenever an Initiate gives out knowledge from his store of Wisdom, harm doth befall those who reject this message. Thus, because of the vow of silence which is imposed upon Initiates, and the unreadiness of the people to receive the Sacred Teachings, the Illuminati must observe caution even though they are, at times, forced to withdraw from society.

In the legend of Freemasonry we are informed that the Master-Builder, Hiram Abiff, met an untimely end because he would not give the Master's "Sacred Word" to the unqualified workmen.

History abounds with biographies of great souls that have suffered martyrdom, because they gave to the unqualified masses greater and higher phases of truth than these latter were able to understand. It is realized that the majority of mankind is yet undeveloped, and those that have evolved fully their mental faculties, are in most cases not interested in the spiritual side of life, because of which the "Masters of the Wisdom" must ever remain in obscurity until humanity is morally and mentally fit to receive the great Truths they have to offer.

"My life you can have, my integrity, never!" were the words that dropped from the lips of Hiram, the dying Master-Builder. Yea, and these same words have been re-uttered from the lips of every dying martyr that has shed his blood for a Principle.

Glorious have been the lives of all those having attained initiation and no one except the most ignorant, or a "dyed-in-the-wool" orthodox Christian, could look at some of the Dieties of primitive man, sculptured in marble or stone, and label the people of those periods illiterate savages. It is only the most bigoted person who could behold the stern, yet tranquil features of the meditating Buddhas, and not perceive the ideals for which the GREAT ONE stood.

Not until the aspirant is able to see that all religions are fundamentally the same,—not until he regards the human family as the offspring from one Divine Father,—not until he has developed these faculties, can he consider himself qualified to enter the path of esoteric training. The pupil may, however, rest assured that if he endeavors to cultivate such qualities, he will necessarily attract the attention of a teacher, who will accelerate the atomic vibrations of his vehicles and put him in touch with the superphysical realms, so that he may qualify himself to become an independent investigator, thereby becoming a true helper of humanity.

It must not be supposed that to become a spiritual helper the aspirant should neglect his material duties. The ancient adage, "When you are in Rome, do as the Romans do," emphasizes a phase of occult truth. In India, where the people seem to readily respond to the inner urge,—when one hears the inner voice and answers the call,—his relatives and associates usually consider it their duty to assist him in every possible manner. But in the western world the reverse situation confronts the aspirant and when he heeds the call, he is destined to suffer (if not sufficiently strong) in his effort to repel the onslaught of thoughts that will be hurled against him.

It must be conceded that since Gautama thought it wise to institute the "Middle Path" for a race of people inherently spiritual, the same doctrine should be helpful for the races that are going through the densest phases of materialism. As a matter of fact, the "Middle Path" simply means a rounded development; hence, during the early part of one's unfoldment, material duties need not be neglected, and if one takes up the study of occultism from the viewpoint of the "Middle Path," the knowledge acquired should make him more efficient in coping with the duties of every day life, and the quintessence of this knowledge will be absorbed as pabulum to further his spiritual evolution.

I have casually met, and am acquainted with many men and women in business life, who although not in the least interested in religion are, nevertheless, physically, mentally, and spiritually in advance of many of the hierophants of religious organizations, and are, as a matter of fact, mentally and morally superior to many lecturers and teachers of modern psychology.

The teachings of the "Masters of the Wisdom" are based absolutely on the doctrine of the "Middle Path,"—resulting in the development of "a Sane Mind, a Soft Heart, and a Sound Body." To impress on the students' minds the sacredness of material duties, the followers of the Elder Brothers of the Rose Cross are instructed to chant at devotional services, and at esoteric gatherings:

> 'Let's strive to know that we may do,
> What lifts, ennobles, is right and true,
> With love to all and hate to none,
> Let's shun no duty that should be done.
> For knowing how to act aright
> And doing it from morn 'till night.
> From day to day and year to year
> We conquer self and sin and fear."

I have frequently been told by people who seem to possess keen mental faculties (and who would be greatly appreciated in schools of metaphysics), that their disinclination to take up the study of occult science was due to the teachings of a philosophy which might cause one to become abnormal and eccentric, and in many instances, might be the cause of complete physical affliction.

It cannot be denied that there are many queer

specimens of lecturers and teachers on the platform, as well as their students, who claim to possess wonderful occult powers; since men are judged by their works, as trees are judged by their fruits, those that are unable to reason from effect to cause, are, in nearly all instances, prone to conclude that the queerness and physical affliction of both teachers and pupils have been brought about because of the fact that they are students of spiritual science.

My dear reader! such is not the case. If the credulous masses were in possession of the mere rudiments of the Sacred Science, they, instead of ignoring Occult Teachings, would understand that the lecturers and students referred to above as "queer," and those physically afflicted, have brought these conditions upon themselves,—having taken up with the Holy Science from purely selfish motives, accompanied by a corresponding failure to live in accordance with the "Doctrine of the Middle Path."

Through eagerness to acquire occult knowledge, many have paid pseudo-occult teachers fabulous prices for courses which are represented to contain special instructions for the unfoldment of occult powers.

Because of the ardent, selfish desires of those who are seeking, a few have succeeded in prematurely awakening the latent forces; but not having been instructed in the absolute necessity of living the chaste life (the only means by which the highest aspect of the Will can be developed), they lack the controlling force, and like a ship without the rudder on the stormy ocean, they are buffeted about by the merciless subtle forces of Nature, which have innocently perhaps, but certainly selfishly, or ignorantly been awakened.

It is regrettable to note that the majority of those who do take up the study of Spiritual Science, and who begin such study late in life, are, almost always doing so, only as a last resort in their quest for a solution of the many paradoxes of daily life. As long as they can possibly sing:
"When all the world is young, lad,
    And all the trees are green,
  And every goose a swan, lad,
    And every lass a queen,"—
or, until material conditions force them to take such a step, never do they give a moment's thought to the psychic side of life. As one philosophical lecturer jokingly expressed: "We respond to the spiritual hunch, only after we have drained dry the wine bottle of life,—or when the right foot is in the grave, and the left is on a banana peel." Persons not interested in the spiritual side of life, are disqualified to reason from "effect to cause" and vice versa.

It is evident that since they have not been instructed in Occult Science, they cannot differentiate between the positive mystic, who has entered the path at an early age and has given the best days of his life in the development of the HEAD

AND HEART, and him, who has ignorantly taken up occult studies as a last resort and has been delving in psychic phenomena with the selfish purpose of acquiring assistance in his quest for material gain.

Nature has wisely kept from the unworthy the secrets pertaining to the unseen forces of the universe, while on the other hand, Her zealous Messengers,—the Custodians of the Mysteries,—are ever anxious to swing ajar the door of the Temple of Wisdom to any one mentally and morally fit.

Carefully ponder over the following timely warning given in occult parlance to the candidate, who seeks admittance:

> "Search for the Paths. But, O Lanoo, be of clean heart before thou startest on thy journey. Before thou takest thy first step, learn to discern the real from the false, the ever-fleeting from the ever-lasting. Learn above all to separate head-learning from soul-wisdom, the "eye" from the "heart" doctrine."

If the candidate seeking admittance possesses the requirements as quoted, he has nothing to fear; but if a single selfish motive lurks in his heart, the swing of the pendulum will bring a reaction equivalent to his motive,—yea, he will be forced back to the duties of the outer world until he has made himself worthy to approach the sacred sanctuary. Thus the Ancient Antillean adage, "He that desires to suck milk from the breast of the virgin mother Nany must be parching with thirst, and have no teeth to bite." Unless one is hungering and thirsting after righteousness, NEVER WILL Nature seveal to him her secrets.

It must be remembered that after Gautama attained enlightenment, he thought it unwise to teach the "Norm" (The Higher Truth) to the credulous masses. History informs us that the Wise One instituted the "Middle Path" ONLY after he had been implored by Bramā Sahampati, the Great Deva, "to preach the truth for the sake of the few, but for the profit of the many."

It is now over twenty-six hundred years since the "Middle Path" has been instituted; and although it is obvious that man is but of a few days and is full of trouble, yet we find the majority of humanity clinging as tenaciously as of yore to the "loaves and fishes," and appearing perfectly satisfied to be continually deceived by the fleeting joys of mundane existence.

Over twenty-six hundred years have elapsed since Gautama trod the banks of the Ganges, to teach truths to the Aryans; and during this long interim there have been but few willing to accept the training designed to prepare Neophytes for esoteric instruction; consequently only a slight extension of the imagination is needed to convince oneself why the great Reformer was apprehensive about teaching his contemporaries the "Norm of Norms."

It is an accepted belief among all students of the Ancient Wisdom Religion, that the egos now functioning in Aryan race bodies, once inhabited vehicles of the Lemurian and Atlantean races, and it is also recognized that the bodies of primitive races are extremely dense; but that very density rendered the spirits more immune from the physical and mental impacts which these races underwent during their struggles for existence.

Since the vehicles of the primitive races were wholly undeveloped, it is perfectly clear that the egos functioning in such bodies could not as readily respond to mental impacts as could the egos reincarnated in high-strung Aryan race bodies. Thus for psychological and physiological reasons the wise leaders, whom we call "The Masters of the Wisdom," instituted special occult instructions to suit the various grades of evolving beings. The saying: "Western Methods for Western peoples," is based on inviolable laws which govern occult chemistry; and he who ignorantly or wilfully violates the simplest of these laws, can never escape the consequences.

The astrological impression concerning the "Seven Planetary Genii," and the Bible reference to the "Seven Spirits Before the Throne," are certainly not mere idle phantasies for, in occult philosophies, the Seven Schools of the Lesser

"CAR OF THE NORM"

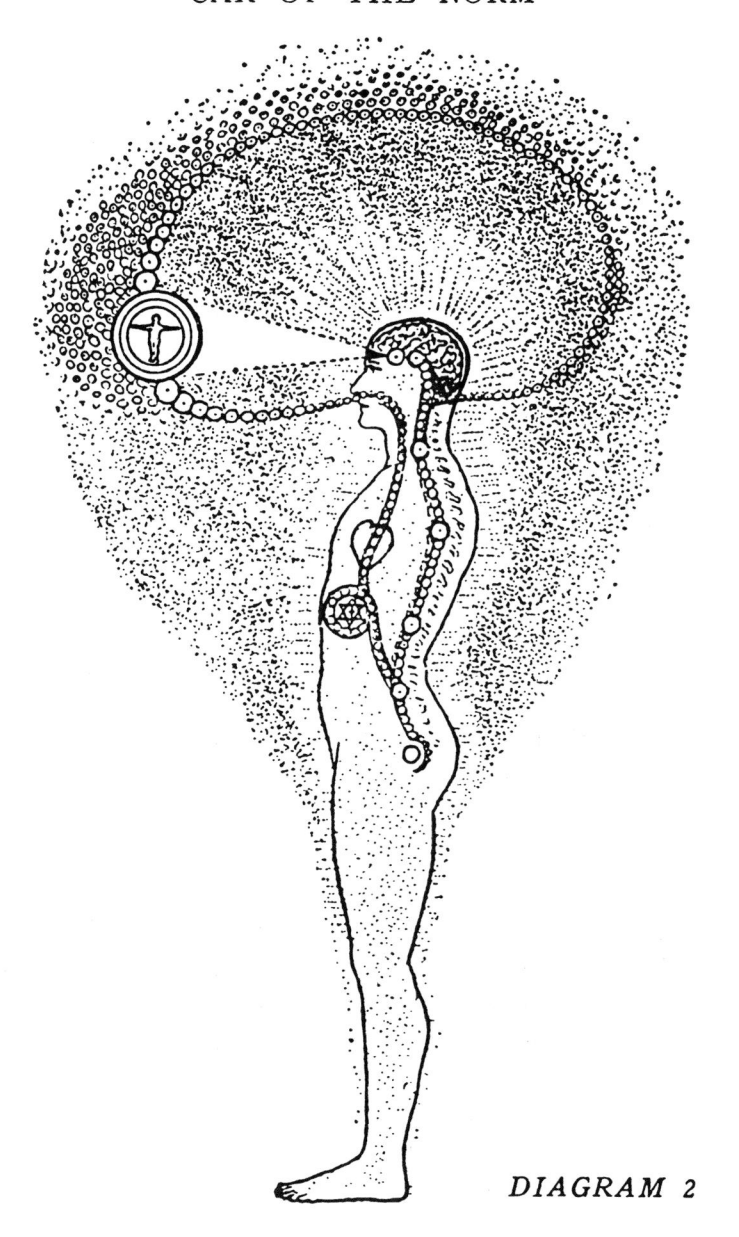

DIAGRAM 2

Mysteries are also spoken of, and, when analyzed from the esoteric point of view, these various statements have identically the same meaning.

Although exoteric exercises are given by each school to suit the needs of the egos evolving through them, such exercises are, nevertheless, insufficient to suit the pioneers who have forged ahead of their compatriots, and to render these souls additional help, the custodians of the Sacred Mysteries (who are our Elder Brothers) have instituted individual esoteric exercises which are in absolute harmony with the keynote of each aspirant.

History informs us that Pythagoras admonished his students—"Never suffer sleep to close thy eyelids after thy going to bed, till thou hast examined by thy reason all thy actions of the day. Wherein have I done amiss? What have I done? What have I omitted that I ought to have done? If in this examination thou findest that thou hast done amiss, reprimand thyself severely for it, and if thou hast done any good,—rejoice!"

Identically the same exercise is given to exoteric students of the Western Wisdom School. But in harmony with the rules and regulations governing all occult schools, the ray to which each disciple is attuned is withheld; other esoteric instructions are likewise withheld until the aspirant has proven himself worthy and well qualified.

Let it be strictly understood that in occultism

there is no favoritism, and those having received individual instructions have merited them.

Hear again, oh reader! another of the inviolable rules to which every teacher of the Sacred Science adheres: "Never will he use occult powers to convince others of the spiritual life, nor will he charge for advice or esoteric instructions." As a matter of fact, those that have forged ahead and are qualified to render spiritual help well know of the grave responsibilities resting upon their shoulders.

In the "Mahatma Letters" to A. P. Sinnett, the Master declared, "Adepts, too, make mistakes." In occult literature it is said that, should a teacher awaken a pupil prematurely, he would be responsible for the evolution of the ego. It can readily be seen that such a candidate would be a source of trouble to the teacher, because the time which would have been to a degree misspent on one individual, could have been more constructively used otherwise. Thus arose the adage: "The teacher delays his own eternal happiness by each new pupil he takes unto himself." The foregoing statement must however be taken figuratively only, for, in the great scheme of things, time is never wasted. Nevertheless, there is much truth in such an adage, for we do know that the Great Ones are very cautious in taking on new pupils. Those that have been so fortunate as to receive special help should be ever loyal to their teachers. Yea, while writing these words, the writer has reobligated himself to do more for the good of furthering the cause of Universal Brotherhood, because by so doing, he—as all disciples should—is showing loyalty both to the teacher, and to the principle which each espouses.

This point is clearly illustrated as is shown in another volume previously published, the title of which is, "Steps to Self-Mastery," wherein the author has mentioned how he was assisted by a lay-brother of the Rosicrucian Order. It is also recited in that work how Philip, the Christian Initiate, helped the eunuch of Ethiopia. Likewise, it is found in "Old Diary Leaves" of the Theosophical Society, that Colonel Olcott mentioned how the Master Morya visited him, after which the whole trend of the Colonel's life was changed. This practical business man being so impressed, gave up all material pursuits to selflessly serve mankind until the end of his days.

There are incidents recorded which show that the mere touch of the Master was sufficient to assist the candidate. Such was the case of Vivekananda, but in nearly all such instances the Great Ones helped their disciples while thousands of miles away, and under no circumstances was gold demanded. If aspirants to spiritual knowledge would exert themselves and apply but a phase of "Reason's Torch," they could at once detect the true teachers from the false ones.

My dear reader! "Cosmic Law works for him

who works with it." Like the Hebrew Prophet, Elijah, who waited on the raven to bring him food, true occult teachers give all they have of courage and of cheer, and wait upon Nature (The Raven), to feed them. Thus it is only a pretense to say that, the teacher must charge in order to be able to meet his material obligations.

"When the student is ready, the teacher appears," is the adage of every occult society. But let this be impressed deeply on the mind that, READINESS does not necessarily mean the renouncing of one's material duties, nor in the reading of books, nor dreaming away the time in silent meditation.

Max Heindel, who founded the Rosicrucian Fellowship, urged his students to "Shun no duty that should be done," and that is the method adopted by the Western Wisdom School, which is a ray from the Rosicrucian Order. He who endeavors to fulfil his material duties, and loves universally, has fulfilled the law. For instance, the author's own personal experience may be of help in throwing light on the subject. Although he hungered and thirsted after righteousness, he did not shun his material duties. He had little time at his disposal to give to the reading of metaphysical books, and was therefore obliged to remain in his particular sphere of activity until conditions were so adjusted that he could give his undivided attention to spiritual work.

During the aeons of time it has taken man to accomplish his material duties, he has been building a new vehicle, whether consciously or unconsciously, which is known to esoteric Christians as the "Golden Wedding Garment."

Oliver Wendell Holmes referred to this glorious vehicle in his beautiful poem, "The Chambered Nautilus," in these words:

"Build thee more stately mansions, O my soul!
As the swift seasons roll!"

Yea, the evolved man may be likened to a caterpillar, which through the slow process of metamorphosis has built the more complex body of a butterfly, which is bedecked in iridescent hue. But, as the fully matured butterfly must of itself break through the walls of the cocoon before it can test its wings, in like manner the man who is fast evolving out of matter, will some day soar away in the glorious vehicle which he has built. Gautama Buddha called it the "Car of the Norm." (See Diagram 2.)

Due to the age in which we are now living, the author has deemed it fitting to now designate this intangible garment,—Man's Gasless Aeroplane which he has attempted to portray in Diagram 2. This portrayal was first given to the world in a previous publication of this author, reference to which has before been made, and known as "Steps to Self-Mastery." Thus in the words of the Buddha:

"Whoso the Faith and Wisdom hath attained—
His states of mind, well-harnessed, lead him on.
Conscience the pole, and Mind the yoke thereof,
And Heedfulness the watchful charioteer:
The furnishments of Righteousness, the Car:
Rapture the axle, Energy the wheels,
And Calm, yokefellow of the Balanced Mind:
Desirelessness the drapery thereof:
Goodwill and Harmlessness his weapons are,
Together with Detachment of the mind.
Endurance is the armour of the Norm,
And to attain the Peace that car rolls on.
'Tis built by self, by one's own self becometh—
This chariot, incomparable, supreme:
Seated therein the sages leave the world,
And verily they win the victory."

THE END